K. E. VONN

Beginner's Guide To The Apocalypse

A Practical Overview of the Book of Revelation–
Chapter by Chapter

Contents

Join the K.E. Vonn Mailing List

If you enjoy this resource, let the author know you're interested in reading potential upcoming books in the Beginner's Guide series. https://www.subscribepage.com/KEVonnLanding

Revelation - Introduction

Seasoned Christians and new believers alike continue to be puzzled by the last book in the Bible. Revelation was written by the Apostle John, a disciple of Jesus, while exiled to the island of Patmos. It is filled with symbolism, strange creatures, and seemingly undecipherable future events. So why would anyone attempt to write a book on Revelation? Shouldn't we leave this task to the scholars and prophetic sages of the world?

But that's just it, John did not write this book for an audience of scholars but for a varied body of believers young and old, rich and poor, schooled and unschooled. Maybe it's not so complicated or confusing. Maybe it just is what it is. John saw something fantastical and he wrote it down—not John the scholar. John, the fisherman turned apostle. And what he was shown at the time pertained to events that were so far into the future that he couldn't have had any frame of reference to accurately tell us what these things were because he really didn't know what he was seeing.

So you see, the best person to write on Revelation is not a scholar, but a person who is living in the time John described. Someone who could readily identify what John was seeing because they were, in fact, seeing the same things. We are living in a time that is quickly rushing to match the end time events. After years spent as a student of the Bible, there are many symbols and events in Revelation, which were baffling, that I now recognize and understand. Perhaps things are clearer because the events from those pages are now here. The insight of the most respected Biblical scholar that lived one hundred, even fifty years ago, has nothing on the average believer living in the 21st century.

For example, can you imagine having a vision of the LAX airport in the 1800s?

> *"I saw giant birds with wing spans of 200 feet! They were metallic creatures. They made a noise like thunder and fire came out of their wings. They nest near houses of glass and people inside have telepathic powers. Some choose to step to one side and let their telepathic powers move them along as if they are floating close to the ground."*

You get the picture. Do we really need a scholar or someone with prophetic insight to interpret this vision? No, we just need to live in the age of airplanes and people movers - something most of us take for granted when we travel. So, what did John see? He saw a future that was much different; and he saw the throne room of God - something that will never be common and ordinary, no matter what time period.

I am not going to pull out a bunch of reference books and biblical texts to exegete the passages. No. I am going to simply look around, and with the help of the most knowledgeable scholar (the Holy Spirit), I am going to take the things I can recognize in my generation to determine where we are in this future event. Don't misunderstand, I am not trying to find the day and hour that Jesus is coming back. Wouldn't that be a silly waste of time since he told us we would never know? However, I am going to look closely at the season. To paraphrase, Jesus said, "You don't know exactly when but you should be watching, praying, and expecting my return when you see the signs." And thankfully his disciples never forgot what he said.

Matthew 24:32-33

> *Now learn this parable from the fig tree: When its branch has already become tender and puts forth leaves, you know that summer is near.* **So you also, when you see all these things, know that it is near—at the doors!**

Luke 21:34-36

> *But take heed to yourselves, lest your hearts be weighed down with carousing, drunkenness, and cares of this life, and that Day come on you unexpectedly. For it will come as a snare on all those who dwell on the face of the whole earth.* **Watch therefore, and pray always that you may be counted worthy to escape all these things that will come to pass, and to stand before the Son of Man.**

Even Paul said in 1 Thessalonians 5:1-7

> *But concerning the times and the seasons, brethren, you have no need that I should write to you. For you yourselves know perfectly that the day of the Lord so comes as a thief in the night. For when they say, "Peace and safety!" then sudden destruction comes upon them, as labor pains upon a pregnant woman. And they shall not escape.* **But you, brethren, are not in darkness, so that this Day should overtake you as a thief. You are all sons of**

light and sons of the day. We are not of the night nor of darkness. Therefore let us not sleep, as others, but let us watch and be sober.

So, here we go. We are about to begin Revelation - one chapter at a time, not for biblical scholars but for beginners who simply want a practical guide to the end of the age.

Revelation - Chapter 1

Revelation 1:1-20 KJV:

The Revelation of Jesus Christ, which God gave unto him, to shew unto his servants things which must shortly come to pass; and he sent and signified it by his angel unto his servant John: 2 Who bare record of the word of God, and of the testimony of Jesus Christ, and of all things that he saw. 3 Blessed is he that readeth, and they that hear the words of this prophecy, and keep those things which are written therein: for the time is at hand. 4 John to the seven churches which are in Asia: Grace be unto you, and peace, from him which is, and which was, and which is to come; and from the seven Spirits which are before his throne; 5 And from Jesus Christ, who is the faithful witness, and the first begotten of the dead, and the prince of the kings of the earth. Unto him that loved us, and washed us from our sins in his own blood, 6 And hath made us kings and priests unto God and his Father; to him be glory and dominion for ever and ever. Amen. 7 Behold, he cometh with clouds; and every eye shall see him, and they also which pierced him: and all kindreds of the earth shall wail because of him.

Even so, Amen. **8** *I am Alpha and Omega, the beginning and the ending, saith the Lord, which is, and which was, and which is to come, the Almighty.* **9** *I John, who also am your brother, and companion in tribulation, and in the kingdom and patience of Jesus Christ, was in the isle that is called Patmos, for the word of God, and for the testimony of Jesus Christ.* **10** *I was in the Spirit on the Lord's day, and heard behind me a great voice, as of a trumpet,* **11** *Saying, I am Alpha and Omega, the first and the last: and, What thou seest, write in a book, and send it unto the seven churches which are in Asia; unto Ephesus, and unto Smyrna, and unto Pergamos, and unto Thyatira, and unto Sardis, and unto Philadelphia, and unto Laodicea.* **12** *And I turned to see the voice that spake with me. And being turned, I saw seven golden candlesticks;* **13** *And in the midst of the seven candlesticks one like unto the Son of man, clothed with a garment down to the foot, and girt about the paps with a golden girdle.* **14** *His head and his hairs were white like wool, as white as snow; and his eyes were as a flame of fire;* **15** *And his feet like unto fine brass, as if they burned in a furnace; and his voice as the sound of many waters.* **16** *And he had in his right hand seven stars: and out of his mouth went a sharp two-edged sword: and his countenance was as the sun shineth in his strength.* **17** *And when I saw him, I fell at his feet as dead. And he laid his right hand upon me, saying unto me, Fear not; I am the first and the last:* **18** *I am he that liveth, and was dead; and, behold, I am alive for evermore, Amen; and have the keys of hell and of death.* **19** *Write the things which thou hast seen, and the things which are, and the* *things which shall be hereafter;* **20** *The mystery of the seven stars which thou sawest in my right hand, and the seven golden candlesticks. The seven stars are the angels of the seven churches: and the seven candlesticks which thou sawest are the seven churches.*

It was a loud voice behind him - like an unexpected trumpet blast which said, "WRITE ON A SCROLL WHAT YOU SEE AND SEND IT TO THE SEVEN CHURCHES: TO EPHESUS, SMYRNA, PERGAMUM, THYATIRA, SARDIS, PHILADEL-PHIA AND LAODICEA" Startled by what he hears, John, the apostle, turns around to see a fantastic sight - a man walking among seven large candlesticks and holding seven stars in his hand. It's Jesus and he is shining brighter than the sun.

Jesus identifies himself to John, not as the son of man, nor as his old friend and rabbi, but as the alpha and the omega. The way the scripture is worded, John doesn't seem to even recognize him. Jesus is like a king who goes among his people dressed as a common man and then that common man is seen again dressed in his royal robes with all the pomp and circumstance. Like the TV program, Undercover Boss. When the boss reveals who he is, employees are shocked, reverent, and a little afraid of what they said when they didn't realize who he was.

Jesus went undercover when he came to earth the first time. He accepted dinner invitations, he healed people of terminal diseases, he laughed, he cried, he cooked. He was God among us. Hidden in plain sight. But he is not hiding who he is anymore. He did what he came to earth to do - take the punishment for the sins of humankind. And now when we see him, we shall

3

see him as he really is - the King over all kings and the Lord over all lords. The beginning and the end. No wonder John was overwhelmed and without strength when he saw him. He doesn't say, "When I turned around my pal Jesus was standing there." This man was now terrifyingly formal in his description of his friend. And, when we see him, whether we love him or hate him, we too will be in awe of his majesty.

John didn't just bow at his feet when he saw Jesus, he fell like a dead man. His body, his soul, his spirit couldn't take all that majesty and he went down with his face to the ground. Jesus touched him. He spoke tenderly to him. He said, *"Don't be afraid! Though I am the First and Last, the Living One who died, who is now alive forevermore, who has the keys of hell and death—don't be afraid! Write down what you have just seen and what will soon be shown to you."*

Now that he has shown John who he really is under the fleshly garment he wore on earth, Jesus wants to show John what his church looks like. How fascinating that the God of all the universe, the beginning and the end of all things, is walking among believers, actively involved in everything that is going on. He's not far away but very near. According to John he holds the leaders of his church in the palm of his hand - now that's close. We should be encouraged and a little frightened that God is so close to our everyday. It should cause us to be more "God-conscious" and less "self-conscious."

What was the purpose of this encounter? To give John a revelation (an unveiling, a disclosure) of what he was seeing and what was to come in the future. It wasn't to confuse but to give clarity. John confidently claims that his book is a dictated revelation given to him from the living, breathing Word of God - Jesus. He promises a special blessing for those who read the revelation aloud, listen to it and keep those things which are written in it. Believers know that a blessing is already on the word of God as a whole. If you read it, listen to it and do what it says, there's no way you won't be blessed. After all, to read, listen to, or do what the word of God says is to read, listen to and do what Jesus said. So, why a "special" blessing on this particular book?

Like all the various composers of the Bible, John couldn't have known the scope of his own words— how far down the church would travel. Perhaps the special blessing on reading and listening to Revelation was to motivate the followers of Christ to push past the veiled references that are really not all that black and white - to keep reading until what they see in the book is happening all around them. I heard an end-time scholar say that if Revelation had been an easy read it would have never gotten off the Island of Patmos where John wrote it. It would have been confiscated and destroyed. But as it stands the average unbeliever will find nothing of interest in the book of Revelation - it is madness to anyone who doesn't have some desire for God.

Or, perhaps the meaning of this special blessing on Revelation is meant to intensify with time, as the signs draw nearer and the end closes in on us. It is for those who will be in the worst possible earthly situation there has been and ever will be, according to Jesus. Perhaps a warning to not give up hope of salvation because of what we see around us. It is to recognize the events that will culminate into the wrath of God on anyone who either directly or indirectly opposes him and his son, declaring that they don't need a Savior.

Before John shares his vision, he makes a strong declaration - JESUS IS COMING BACK. He reinforced the words that Jesus himself spoke about when describing his return. John says, *"Behold, he is coming with clouds and every eye will see him, even they who pierced him. And all the tribes of the earth will mourn because of him."*

Can you imagine just an ordinary person on an ordinary day? On your way to work, traffic backed up as usual. Mentally assessing your to do list. And then it happens. Your worst nightmare - a thunderous sound that shakes your bones and pierces your eardrums. A sound that could wake the dead. You look up and the one whom you have denied even existed, the one whose name you used as a curse word, has split the sky and is visible to everyone in all his glory with a host of angels. You scream in your mind, "This can't be real, I thought it was a fairy tale, this can't be happening!" Every eye, believer and non-believer, Jew and Gentile will see him. And those who did not believe will mourn at the sight of him.

Jesus gets no pleasure in meeting like this. He would rather that all be expecting him. Excited to see him. Not caught up in the worldly affairs or turmoil that has engulfed the culture but prepared for his return. That is why he has appeared to John. To tell him to tell us what the end of the last days will look like so we won't be caught unaware. But before He talks about what's to come, he gives John messages to his believers - his church.

Revelation - Chapter 2

Revelation 2:1-28 KJV:

Unto the angel of the church of Ephesus write; These things saith he that holdeth the seven stars in his right hand, who walketh in the midst of the seven golden candlesticks; 2 I know thy works, and thy labour, and thy patience, and how thou canst not bear them which are evil: and thou hast tried them which say they are apostles, and are not, and hast found them liars: 3 And hast borne, and hast patience, and for my name's sake hast laboured, and hast not fainted. 4 Nevertheless I have somewhat against thee, because thou hast left thy first love. 5 Remember therefore from whence thou art fallen, and repent, and do the first works; or else I will come unto thee quickly, and will remove thy candlestick out of his place, except thou repent. 6 But this thou hast, that thou hatest the deeds of the Nicolaitanes, which I also hate. 7 He that hath an ear, let him hear what the Spirit saith unto the churches; To him that overcometh will I give to eat of the tree of life, which is in the midst of the paradise of God. 8 And unto the angel of the church in Smyrna write; These things saith the first and the last, which was dead, and is alive; 9 I know thy works, and tribulation, and poverty, (but thou art rich) and I know the blasphemy of them which say they are Jews, and are not, but are the synagogue of Satan. 10 Fear none of those things which thou shalt suffer: behold, the devil shall cast some of you into prison, that ye may be tried; and ye shall have tribulation ten days: be thou faithful unto death, and I will give thee a crown of life. 11 He that hath an ear, let him hear what the Spirit saith unto the churches; He that overcometh shall not be hurt of the second death. 12 And to the angel of the church in Pergamos write; These things saith he which hath the sharp sword with two edges; 13 I know thy works, and where thou dwellest, even where Satan's seat is: and thou holdest fast my name, and hast not denied my faith, even in those days wherein Antipas was my faithful martyr, who was slain among you, where Satan dwelleth. 14 But I have a few things against thee, because thou hast there them that hold the doctrine of Balaam, who taught Balac to cast a stumblingblock before the children of Israel, to eat things sacrificed unto idols, and to commit fornication. 15 So hast thou also them that hold the doctrine of the Nicolaitanes, which thing I hate. 16 Repent; or else I will come unto thee quickly, and will fight against them with the sword of my mouth. 17 He that hath an ear, let him hear what the Spirit saith unto the churches; To him that overcometh will I give to eat of the hidden manna, and will give him a white stone, and in the stone a new name written, which no man knoweth saving he that receiveth it. 18 And unto the angel of the church in Thyatira write; These things saith the Son of

God, who hath his eyes like unto a flame of fire, and his feet are like fine brass 19 I know thy works, and charity, and service, and faith, and thy patience, and thy works; and the last to be more than the first. 20 Notwithstanding I have a few things against thee, because thou sufferest that woman Jezebel, which calleth herself a prophetess, to teach and to seduce my servants to commit fornication, and to eat things sacrificed unto idols. 21 And I gave her space to repent of her fornication; and she repented not. 22 Behold, I will cast her into a bed, and them that commit adultery with her into great tribulation, except they repent of their deeds. 23 And I will kill her children with death; and all the churches shall know that I am he which searcheth the reins and hearts: and I will give unto every one of you according to your works. 24 But unto you I say, and unto the rest in Thyatira, as many as have not this doctrine, and which have not known the depths of Satan, as they speak; I will put upon you none other burden. 25 But that which ye have already hold fast till I come. 26 And he that overcometh, and keepeth my works unto the end, to him will I give power over the nations: 27 And he shall rule them with a rod of iron; as the vessels of a potter shall they be broken to shivers: even as I received of my Father. 28 And I will give him the morning star. 29 He that hath an ear, let him hear what the Spirit saith unto the churches.

Before Jesus shows John the end time events he dictates letters to John to the seven churches (actually communities) in what is modern day Turkey. These communities would have been started by Jewish believers in Jesus and would have been comprised of not only Jews but Gentiles as well - the one new man that is spoken of in the scriptures (Ephesians 2:14-18). Obviously, these were not all the communities of believers that existed at the time but perhaps Jesus chose these seven as a representation of the church body as a whole, with each one having a unique set of issues.

The first church Jesus addresses is the church at Ephesus. Paul, the apostle wrote letters to this church. The book of Ephesians gives us a glimpse of their strong love and faith in Jesus. However, by the time John is transcribing this letter, this community needs some strong directive. Jesus basically says *I know* your works, your labor, your patience but you have left your first love. Work, labor, patience are all important but Jesus is most concerned with their relationship with him while doing those things. He corrects them and tells them that if they will remain faithful, they will eat fruit from the tree of life.

Smyrna is the second church that Jesus addresses. He tells them, "*I know* how much you suffer for me. I know your poverty (yet you are rich) but stop being afraid of what you are about to suffer." He tells them they will spend ten days in prison. Most of us would tremble at the thought - how is this encouraging? Well, considering that they probably thought if they got arrested, they would be there for life. Jesus's words would have been most comforting, "No, it's only going to be a few days." Jesus told them that if they remained faithful, they would not have to worry about the second death - the eternal death.

The third church Jesus addresses is Pergamum. Jesus says, "*I know* that you live where satan's throne is and yet you remain loyal to me but you tolerate sexual sin among you" Yes, they lived where satan felt comfortably at home. There was a ginormous alter to Zeus in Pergamum. The worship of false gods almost always accompany a tolerance of sexual sin. However, if they were victorious over their cultural influence, Jesus promised they would eat of the hidden manna that the children of Israel ate in the wilderness back in the day. They would also receive a white stone with a new name.

For the church in Thyatira he said. "*I know* your good deeds and kindness to the poor. I see your faith and patience but you are permitting that women Jezebel to teach leniency in adultery and perversion and that eating meat sacrificed to idols is okay." There are consequences for purposely discounting what God says is harmful saying things like, "What's the big deal?" or "That's not so bad." And to be sure, the most damaging sin that satan uses to destroy people is sexual sin. He wants to corrupt the purpose for sex that God intended - for a man and a woman to produce godly offspring in a loving relationship. Those who don't get drawn away by their lusts will be given power to rule nations - presumably when Jesus returns. Jesus tells them he will also give them the morning star.

Can you see the pattern in each one of these church bodies? Jesus told John to tell them "I know" what is going on. One thing we can be sure of is that in the last of the last days Jesus will be just as involved in our lives as he was in the former days. Jesus gave each community instructions on how to get back on track (except for the church of Philadelphia, which he did not find anything to correct) and he then promised them a reward. Yes, a reward for remaining faithful to him up to the end.

Why a reward for doing something that they should have already been doing? Because living a life in the complete opposite direction of the culture is difficult. And in the last of the last days it will challenge the most faithful of followers.

What our spiritual senses are bombarded with requires a strong pushback from the apostasy all around us. There will be an increase of injustice, murder, and the like. Look at the nature of humankind according to Paul in 2 Timothy 3:1-5 *"But know this, that in the last days perilous times will come: For men will be lovers of themselves, lovers of money, boasters, proud, blasphemers, disobedient to parents, unthankful, unholy, unloving, unforgiving, slanderers, without self-control, brutal, despisers of good, traitors, headstrong, haughty, lovers of pleasure rather than lovers of God, having a form of godliness but denying its power."*

The perilous times are a result of an "increase" in the depravity of humanity - something that is happening right before our eyes, Rewards will be very appropriate for those amid the psychological, physical and spiritual turmoil.

Revelation - Chapter 3

Revelation 3:1-22 KJV:

And unto the angel of the church in Sardis write; These things saith he that hath the seven Spirits of God, and the seven stars; I know thy works, that thou hast a name that thou livest, and art dead. 2 Be watchful, and strengthen the things which remain, that are ready to die: for I have not found thy works perfect before God. 3 Remember therefore how thou hast received and heard, and hold fast, and repent. If therefore thou shalt not watch, I will come on thee as a thief, and thou shalt not know what hour I will come upon thee. 4 Thou hast a few names even in Sardis which have not defiled their garments; and they shall walk with me in white: for they are worthy. 5 He that overcometh, the same shall be clothed in white raiment; and I will not blot out his name out of the book of life, but I will confess his name before my Father, and before his angels. 6 He that hath an ear, let him hear what the Spirit saith unto the churches. 7 And to the angel of the church in Philadelphia write; These things saith he that is holy, he that is true, he that hath the key of David, he that openeth, and no man shutteth; and shutteth, and no man openeth; 8 I know thy works: behold, I have set before thee an open door, and no man can shut it: for thou hast a little strength, and hast kept my word, and hast not denied my name. 9 Behold, I will make them of the synagogue of Satan, which say they are Jews, and are not, but do lie; behold, I will make them to come and worship before thy feet, and to know that I have loved thee. 10 Because thou hast kept the word of my patience, I also will keep thee from the hour of temptation, which shall come upon all the world, to try them that dwell upon the earth. 11 Behold, I come quickly: hold that fast which thou hast, that no man take thy crown. 12 him that overcometh will I make a pillar in the temple of my God, and he shall go no more out: and I will write upon him the name of my God, and the name of the city of my God, which is new Jerusalem, which cometh down out of heaven from my God: and I will write upon him my new name. 13 He that hath an ear, let him hear what the Spirit saith unto the churches. 14 And unto the angel of the church of the Laodiceans write; These things saith the Amen, the faithful and true witness, the beginning of the creation of God; 15 I know thy works, that thou art neither cold nor hot: I would thou wert cold or hot. 16 So then because thou art lukewarm, and neither cold nor hot, I will spue thee out of my mouth. 17 Because thou sayest, I am rich, and increased with goods, and have need of nothing; and knowest not that thou art wretched, and miserable, and poor, and blind, and naked: 18 I counsel thee to buy of me gold tried in the fire, that thou mayest be rich; and white raiment, that thou mayest be clothed, and that the shame of thy nakedness do not appear; and anoint thine eyes with eyesalve, that thou mayest see. 19 As many as I love, I rebuke and chasten: be zealous therefore, and repent. 20 Behold, I stand at the door, and knock: if any man hear my voice, and open the door, I will come in to him, and will sup with him, and he with me. 21 To him that overcometh will I grant to sit with me in my throne, even as I also overcame, and am set down with my Father in his throne. 22 He that hath an ear, let him hear what the Spirit saith unto the churches.

Jesus further authenticates that he was indeed dictating these letters to John. Every community that received a letter would have surely known that what Jesus was rebuking and encouraging them was true. As a result, this would have given them faith to believe the rest of what John had to say.

Jesus tells the church at Sardis, "*I know* your reputation for being a live and active church but you are dead." They were hypocrites. Jesus told them to go back to what they believed in the beginning. He acknowledged those who hadn't soiled their garments with the world's hypocrisy (the world's filth he called it). They would be clothed in white and their names would never be erased from the Book of Life.

Jesus told the church at Philadelphia, "*I know* you're not strong but you have tried to obey and have not denied my name." Because of that, he was going to open a door for them that no one could shut and force those who were really supporting the cause of satan but claiming to be believers to fall at their feet and acknowledge that they were loved by God. Jesus promised those faithful believers that they would not go through any tribulation, they would be vindicated on earth and they would live in the new Jerusalem. This will make more sense in chapter 21, but the new Jerusalem is a city where God, Jesus, the Holy Spirit and the wife of Jesus will live once the earth is restored.

To Laodicea Jesus said. "*I know* you well. You are neither hot nor cold but lukewarm and I will spit you out of my mouth unless you turn from compromising." They said they were rich but Jesus said they didn't even realize that they were wretched, miserable, poor, blind and naked. He recommended that they buy from him gold tried in the fire (fire represents tests and trials - something that builds character) and garments (which usually represent good deeds or righteous acts). They needed clothes on so they wouldn't be naked and ashamed when they got to heaven - wouldn't that be awful? Everyone in heaven with white robes, or fine linens and they are naked and ashamed because they served themselves the whole time they were on earth. He did promise that everyone that conquered (opened the door to him so he could have input in the decisions they made in the lives) He would allow to sit on the throne with him.

Most of what Jesus promised those who remain faithful is lost in the translation. A white stone with a new name? The morning star? We assume that they are pretty tremendous rewards but for our understanding, it's like giving a toddler a check for a billion dollars - we can't really appreciate the significance. One thing is sure, there will be rewards for those who continue to put what Jesus has said above what the culture is saying.

You might be thinking, "If these are letters to the churches that were existing in John's day, how is that significant to me today?" If there is one thing I have learned from the word of

God, it is that God is comprehensive. Or, as the scriptures declare, "He is the same, yesterday, today, and forevermore." The very fact that there are believers in all parts of the world today speaks of God's ability to relate to us in any age. The message of the gospel translates in every language, culture, and yes, every time period.

Consider this. According to the Bible, approximately 4,000 years ago, God sent Moses to Egypt to demand that Pharaoh, the ruler in Egypt, let the Israelites go - release them from slavery. Most, Americans at least, are familiar with the movie "The Ten Commandments." Well, this is a true event and the account is found in the whole book of Exodus in the Bible. Moses was God's spokesman and he brought Pharaoh God's messages, and plagues when Pharaoh refused to comply. Each time he refused, the plagues became more severe. Finally, the last plague brought the Egyptians to their knees. The firstborn of every person and animal was killed in a single night. However, God had instructed the Israelites to apply the blood of a sinless, spotless, lamb on the doorposts of their home so that anyone inside would be spared that night. This event is called the feast of Passover because death passed over those who were protected by the blood of the lamb.

God later instructed the Israelites to continue to commem-orate this Passover Feast every year as well as six other feasts (four that are celebrated in the springtime and three that are celebrated in the fall), Seven feasts for them to "rehearse" every year: The spring feasts are the *Passover Feast*, the *Feast of Unleavened Bread*, the *Feasts of the First Fruits*, and the *Feast of Pentecost*. The fall feasts are the *Feast of Trumpets*, the *Day of Atoning*, and the *Feast of Tabernacles*. You can read about these feasts in Leviticus chapter 23 and it is fascinating to study their significance.

Fast forward approximately 2,000 years, at a time when 11 disciples are confused and frightened at the events that have just taken place. Judas has betrayed Jesus so that he is arrested and unjustly sentenced to death by crucifixion. Yet Jesus's ministry was predicated on the idea that he was their Messiah, destined to become king of Israel. Was this an unexpected event that caught God and his Son off guard? No. of course not. Jesus, whom John the Baptist had called the "spotless, lamb" was crucified on the day of that *Passover Feast*. The same feast that the Israelites commemorated every year! Jesus was buried on the day of the *Feast of Unleavened Bread.* Jesus rose again on the *Feasts of the First Fruits.* And Jesus sent the Holy Spirit to earth on the day of the *Feast of Pentecost* recorded in Acts 2.

God says or does something in one time period and then fulfills its significance in another time period. That's why some are so tempted to keep predicting when Jesus will come back. If Jesus so completely fulfilled the first four spring feasts that God instituted when he came the first time, surely we should expect him to fulfill the last three fall feasts when he returns. Revelation chapters two and three show us that the Bible is full of these mysteries that have multiple meanings for different generations.

Revelation - Chapter 4

Revelation 4:1-11 KJV:

After this I looked, and, behold, a door was opened in heaven: and the first voice which I heard was as it were of a trumpet talking with me; which said, Come up hither, and I will shew thee things which must be hereafter. 2 And immediately I was in the spirit: and, behold, a throne was set in heaven, and one sat on the throne. 3 And he that sat was to look upon like a jasper and a sardine stone: and there was a rainbow round about the throne, in sight like unto an emerald. 4 And round about the throne were four and twenty seats: and upon the seats I saw four and twenty elders sitting, clothed in white raiment; and they had on their heads crowns of gold. 5 And out of the throne proceeded lightnings and thunderings and voices: and there were seven lamps of fire burning before the throne, which are the seven Spirits of God. 6 And before the throne there was a sea of glass like unto crystal: and in the midst of the throne, and round about the throne, were four beasts full of eyes before and behind. 7 And the first beast was like a lion, and the second beast like a calf, and the third beast had a face as a man, and the fourth beast was like a flying eagle. 8 And the four beasts had each of them six wings about him; and they were full of eyes within: and they rest not day and night, saying, Holy, holy, holy, Lord God Almighty, which was, and is, and is to come. 9 And when those beasts give glory and honour and thanks to him that sat on the throne, who liveth for ever and ever, 10 The four and twenty elders fall down before him that sat on the throne, and worship him that liveth for ever and ever, and cast their crowns before the throne, saying, 11 Thou art worthy, O Lord, to receive glory and honour and power: for thou hast created all things, and for thy pleasure they are and were created.

After Jesus takes care of the family business, John is called to "come up." He finds himself in the midst of God's throne room. What he sees is overwhelming to his senses and he describes as much as his eyes can comprehend. He sees God's throne, and the thrones of 24 elders which are positioned around God's throne. He sees fire, lightening, thunder, and living creatures flying around. There is praise and worship like he has never seen or heard before. The closest he had ever come to such brilliance was on the mount of transfiguration in Matthew 17:1.

John refers to God in an odd way in this chapter, he says "the one who sits on the throne." Perhaps since John had never actually seen God, he did not know what he looked like so he did not want to assume that what he was seeing was God. After all, it was a well-known belief that no one could see God's face and live. So, here John was face to face with someone sitting on the throne. Was he having a conflict in his mind? "If this is God on the throne, I should be dead!" He was right. Isaiah had the same experience when he was taken into the presence of God. And, he saw and heard basically the same thing - the creatures, the voice of thunder, the brilliance. Isaiah wrote:

"In the year that King Uzziah died, I saw the Lord sitting on a throne, high and lifted up, and the train of His robe filled the temple. Above it stood seraphim; each one had six wings: with two he covered his face, with two he covered his feet, and with two he flew. And one cried to another and said: Holy, holy, holy is the Lord of hosts; and the posts of the door were shaken by the voice of him who cried out, and the house was filled with smoke. So I said, "Woe is me for I am undone! Because I am a man of unclean lips, and I dwell in the midst of a people of unclean lips; for my eyes have seen the King. The Lord of hosts."

Many times we assume that whenever we read in the scriptures about otherworldly creatures and unexplainable goings on that these things are symbolic. However, why does the creator have to stay within the limits of our finite minds? Isn't he free to create whatever kind of creatures he wants around his throne? Just because we have not seen them before does not mean they have to be symbolic or don't exist. Here is what John saw:

"And in the midst of the throne, and around the throne, were four living creatures full of eyes in front and in back. ...The four living creatures, each having six wings, were full of eyes around and within. And they do not rest day or night, saying: "Holy, holy, holy, Lord God Almighty, who

21

was and is and is to come!" Whenever the living creatures give glory and honor and thanks to him who sits on the throne, who lives forever and ever, the twenty-four elders fall down before him who sits on the throne and worship him who lives forever and ever, and cast their crowns before the throne, saying: "Thou art worthy, O Lord to receive glory and honor and power; for you created all things and by your will they exist and were created."

The creator of everything that exists has allowed not only John and others to see his throne but 24 humans to be seated, not behind him or beneath his feet but around him. We know they are human because of what Jesus said to 12 of them in Matt 19:2-28: *"Then Peter said to him, 'We left everything to follow you. What will we get out of it?' And Jesus replied, 'When I, the Messiah, shall sit upon my glorious throne in the kingdom, you my disciples shall certainly sit on twelve thrones judging the twelve tribes of Israel.'"* If they are around the throne of God, then perhaps some or all of them are facing him. They can interact with him and he can interact with them. Always. There is absolutely no logical reason for God to be in this kind of relationship with us, except that he wants to be.

When my grand kids were age one, two, and three and I would come over for a visit, we had this ritual of reading books. We'd grab a bunch of books off the shelves and I would sit down in the recliner. David (3) would get on one knee, Paul (2) would get on my other knee, and Sarah (1) would sit in the middle. Sarah loved to just laugh out loud every time we'd turn the page. Paul liked to look at the pictures and point out words and items on the page. He loved to hear my approval, "good job, Paul." or "Wow, you are really smart." David just wanted to be able to read. He noticed each word and the whole time I was reading he was trying to memorize what was on the page so that he can do it again by himself.

Then there was me. I am loving the whole experience. It was physically uncomfortable and intellectually unsatisfying but I wouldn't have traded it for the world. There is absolutely no logical reason for me to be in this kind of relationship with them, except I want to be.

Chapter four is entirely devoted to describing what most readers agree is heaven, namely the throne room, a place that has been visited several times by those most fortunate, but yet enjoys a certain exclusivity within the heavenly realm. It seems to be where heavenly business is conducted. It is also where God shows us his unfathomable acknowledgement of his seemingly inconsequential creation. Humankind - made in his image.

Revelation - Chapter 5

Revelation 5:1-14 KJV:

> And I saw in the right hand of him that sat on the throne
> a book written within and on the backside, sealed with
> seven seals. *2 And I saw a strong angel proclaiming with
> a loud voice, Who is worthy to open the book, and to loose
> the seals thereof? 3 And no man in heaven, nor in earth,
> neither under the earth, was able to open the book, neither
> to look thereon. 4 And I wept much, because no man was
> found worthy to open and to read the book, neither to look
> thereon. 5 And one of the elders saith unto me, Weep not:
> behold, the Lion of the tribe of Judah, the Root of David,
> hath prevailed to open the book, and to loose the seven seals
> thereof. 6 And I beheld, and, lo, in the midst of the throne
> and of the four beasts, and in the midst of the elders, stood
> a Lamb as it had been slain, having seven horns and seven
> eyes, which are the seven Spirits of God sent forth into all
> the earth. 7 And he came and took the book out of the right
> hand of him that sat upon the throne. 8 And when he had
> taken the book, the four beasts and four and twenty elders
> fell down before the Lamb, having every one of them harps,*

and golden vials full of odours, which are the prayers of saints. 9 And they sung a new song, saying, Thou art worthy to take the book, and to open the seals thereof: for thou wast slain, and hast redeemed us to God by thy blood out of every kindred, and tongue, and people, and nation; 10 And hast made us unto our God kings and priests: and we shall reign on the earth. 11 And I beheld, and I heard the voice of many angels round about the throne and the beasts and the elders: and the number of them was ten thousand times ten thousand, and thousands of thousands; 12 Saying with a loud voice, Worthy is the Lamb that was slain to receive power, and riches, and wisdom, and strength, and honour, and glory, and blessing. 13 And every creature which is in heaven, and on the earth, and under the earth, and such as are in the sea, and all that are in them, heard I saying, Blessing, and honour, and glory, and power, be unto him that sitteth upon the throne, and unto the Lamb for ever and ever. 14 And the four beasts said, Amen. And the four and twenty elders fell down and worshipped him that liveth for ever and ever.

An event is about to take place and John is an eyewitness. He sees a scroll in the right hand of the one who sat on the throne and an angel calling for anyone who is worthy to open the scroll, and loose its seals, to come forward. There was no one, according to John, and at that moment he began to weep. It was then that one of the elders reassured him that there was one worthy to open the scroll and remove the seals. That's when John looks up into the midst of the throne and sees a lamb that looked like it had been slain. This lamb takes the scroll out of the right hand of the one on the throne and thus begins exuberant worship and praise by not only the elders but *"ten thousand times ten thousand and thousands and thousands"* of angels, according to John. Blessings and honor are outwardly displayed by all creatures in heaven, earth, and under the earth who are beside themselves with adoration for God and for the one who let himself be slain for the redemption of humankind.

Jesus is showing John what took place, what is taking place and what will take place in heaven. I know it's confusing but it is apparent from scripture that God created time for us. The kingdom of heaven is outside of time. Hebrews 9:26 says Jesus took his blood to the end of the age and presented it before "the one who sits on the throne" thus atoning for the sins of not just those who lived before and during his time on earth but for every person in the future who would ever live and sin on the earth. If at the end of the age God has already been presented with the blood of the lamb that has cleansed us from sin because we have accepted his son as Lord and Savior, why then would we live in condemnation? We should live as people who have been freed from the curse of sin. We are now free NOT to sin.

Some continue to suggest that this freedom we enjoy is freedom to sin without eternal consequences, now that we have accepted Jesus as our Savior. However, the scriptures suggest that if we really believe Jesus is the son of God and are truly grateful for his sacrifice, we won't tolerate sin. So you see, your actions prove whether you love him or not. Jesus said, *"If you love me, you will obey me."* (John 14:23) What you do on earth as one who has been forgiven will absolutely count when we stand before God. Will the things you did on earth - striving with people, being selfish and self-absorbed, doing as you please because you have used Christ as a get out of jail free card, burn

26

up in the fire of God's eternal judgment so that you alone will escape? (1 Corinthians. 3:14-15) Or will the things you did with a pure heart and a desire to please God give you great riches and rewards in heaven?

God loves giving out rewards. He rewards his only begotten son with a name above every name in heaven, on earth, and under the earth so that *"...every knee will bow and every tongue will confess that Jesus is Lord to the glory of God the father"* (Philippians 2). And, he rewards those who practice that same humility in being willing to give up their life, and to listen to and obey his Son in all they do.

Before we move on, let's talk about the elephant (or lamb in this case) in the room. Why are we casually reading about a lamb that appears to have been killed but is walking in the midst of the throne of God and is getting all types of adoration? Why is John not freaked out about that? John didn't appear to have any trouble recounting this scene. Well, if you have read the Bible, gone to church or Sunday school, or gotten ahold of a Christian coloring book, you know that Jesus is associated with being a gentle, humble lamb.

According to John himself, on at least two occasions, John the Baptist said of Jesus, *"Behold, the lamb of God who takes away the sins of the world."* (John 1:29, John 1:36) John was not shocked or confused about this lamb in heaven. He was very familiar with what he was seeing as a spiritual symbolic appearance of Jesus Christ after he returned to heaven - a lamb alive but looking as though he had been slain.

Jesus, the Lamb of God, is now about to open the seals on this scroll that was in the right hand of God. It was common in ancient history to use seals on a scroll to prevent anyone but the intended party from reading it. A king's will or a deed was often written on a scroll and sealed with his ring. A scroll with a seal is the equivalent of a certified letter today. Perhaps this certified letter, so to speak, was indeed a will - his will...for those who inherited it. Hebrews 9:16-17: *Now, if someone dies and leaves a will—a list of things to be given away to certain people when he dies—no one gets anything until it is proved that the person who wrote the will is dead. The will goes into effect only after the death of the person who wrote it. While he is still alive no one can use it to get any of those things he has promised them.* Jesus was his own Executor of his will - presenting himself having died but was afterward alive.

The scroll in the father's hand could have been a will. However, as I read John's account of the events it actually seems to me that this scroll could have just as easily been a deed. A deed to earth and all its inhabitants. We are that scroll that costs him his life to purchase.

So here is my supposition, John is seeing a transaction. God hands Jesus the deed to planet earth, the scroll, the prize. We probably would have thought it was more like a booby-prize but Jesus is thrilled and so are all the angels. Psalm 49:8-9 says that there is not enough wealth in all the earth to redeem one soul to keep it out of hell. That means that all this celebrating was because Jesus had just struck it rich. He had redeemed not one, but a number of souls too vast to count, as we will see later. And, Jesus knew what he was getting before he purchased us. The scripture says, "While we were yet sinners, Christ died for us."

Chapter five introduces us to the heavenly transaction between God and his Son. Jesus now gets to break each of the seven seals to uncover what is going on with this property he purchased with his blood. He is about to see just how the previous owner had used it, and in this case, abused it.

Revelation - Chapter 6

Revelation 6:1-17 KJV:

And I saw when the Lamb opened one of the seals, and I heard, as it were the noise of thunder, one of the four beasts saying, Come and see. *2* And I saw, and behold a white horse: and he that sat on him had a bow; and a crown was given unto him: and he went forth conquering, and to conquer. *3* And when he had opened the second seal, I heard the second beast say, Come and see. *4* And there went out another horse that was red: and power was given to him that sat thereon to take peace from the earth, and that they should kill one another: and there was given unto him a great sword. *5* And when he had opened the third seal, I heard the third beast say, Come and see. And I beheld, and lo a black horse; and he that sat on him had a pair of balances in his hand. *6* And I heard a voice in the midst of the four beasts say, A measure of wheat for a penny, and three measures of barley for a penny; and see thou hurt not the oil and the wine. *7* And when he had opened the fourth seal, I heard the voice of the fourth beast say, Come and see. *8* And I looked, and behold a pale horse: and his name that sat on him was Death, and Hell followed with him. And power was given unto them over the fourth part of the earth, to kill with sword, and with hunger, and with death, and with the beasts of the earth. *9* And when he had opened the fifth seal, I saw under the altar the souls of them that were slain for the word of God, and for the testimony which they held: *10* And they cried with a loud voice, saying, How long, O Lord, holy and true, dost thou not judge and avenge our blood on them that dwell on the earth? *11* And white robes were given unto every one of them; and it was said unto them, that they should rest yet for a little season, until their fellowservants also and their brethren, that should be killed as they were, should be fulfilled. *12* And I beheld when he had opened the sixth seal, and, lo, there was a great earthquake; and the sun became black as sackcloth of hair, and the moon became as blood; *13* And the stars of heaven fell unto the earth, even as a fig tree casteth her untimely figs, when she is shaken of a mighty wind. *14* And the heaven departed as a scroll when it is rolled together; and every mountain and island were moved out of their places. *15* And the kings of the earth, and the great men, and the rich men, and the chief captains, and the mighty men, and every bondman, and every free man, hid themselves in the dens and in the rocks of the mountains; *16* And said to the mountains and rocks, Fall on us, and hide us from the face of him that sitteth on the throne, and from the wrath of the Lamb: *17* For the great day of his wrath is come; and who shall be able to stand?

Chapter six is where things start getting a little cloudy for the average Bible reader. It's also where some scholars start to conjecture about the symbolism and allegorical meaning. Some would claim that because of the content, what we read couldn't possibly be literal or have significance in the physical world. It was simply for reflection and serious thought or musing about the spiritual implications.

While I do have a master's degree, I do not want to suggest that I am a scholar or that I am approaching this text from a scholarly platform. I think it is honorable and commendable to have extensive knowledge and research ability in your field of study. However, I have always taken issue with the attitude of those who say that the writings of common ordinary fishermen and their apprentices could only be understood by degree-holding scholars. With that being said, I want to navigate through these passages as if on a river in an uncharted land - cautiously but looking for those things that are familiar or with which I can identify.

To continue with the supposition in the previous chapter, the scroll that God gives to Jesus could have actually been a deed to earth, that which he gave his life. So, let's look at these next events from that perspective.

When each of the first four seals are opened, one of the four living creatures before the throne says "Come," It is commonly assumed that the creature saying "come" is summoning the horse and rider that John sees and that God is responsible for what they are about to go and do. In fact this interpretation is so prevalent, I doubt you would be able to find very many commentaries suggesting otherwise. But let's consider that the creature is actually calling *John* to come and see, not calling forth horse and riders. Or perhaps calling forth the visual of

32

what is written on the scroll. The opening of the seals don't really trigger the events, they merely reveal the events to Jesus, and John who is now looking over his shoulder. Let's look at what happens when Jesus peels back each seal:

The first seal uncovers the work of a rider on a white horse who has a bow, a crown and goes out and conquers. Okay. Conquers what? If we assume that God is responsible for calling forth and sending out the riders then this makes no sense. However, if we assume that the seals reveal merely what is taking place and not from God then we don't need to know what is being conquered. If the conquering is killing, stealing, and destroying then we know that is the work of satan and human puppets. Conquering could also mean controlling people groups. What if the first seal is revealing what influences have dominated the world since Jesus gained the rights to it, as some end-time prophets suggest? The white horse and rider could be the roman empire that was in control at the time of Jesus's death. The influence of Rome has always been conquest, whether hostile or peaceful. The Roman Catholic Church and the Pope continue to be a prominent influence even today. Google the Pope and everything goes white - white hat, white robe, white pope mobile, white helicopter.

The second seal uncovers the work of a rider on a red horse. This rider caused war - civil and otherwise. He was able to take peace from the earth and cause people to kill each other. These are all works of evil. Jesus said that before his return there would be war and rumors of war, but he does not even remotely suggest that he would be the one creating it. No, it would be a product of men's depraved hearts coupled with satanic influence - as it always has been since the fall. If this red horse was an influence on the world, it could be "Red"

China or communism, as end-time prophets believe. Google communism and everything goes red. Communism has been known for taking away peace through fear and intimidation in many countries - and still does. Under the one child policy, China caused many parents to kill their children if it was a girl or if it was a second child. Under Joseph Stalin alone at least a million people were imprisoned and almost as many were executed.

The third seal uncovers the work of a rider on a black horse. Most of us who have read this have assumed that this rider with a pair of scales in his hand and hearing the voice say "Two pounds of wheat for a day's wages, and six pounds of barley for a day's wages, and do not damage the oil and the wine!" suggests scarcity of food, so much so that the supply is low and the demand is high. I imagine that evidence of scarcity of food would look like what happened in Venezuela - economic and financial crises in various parts of the world. This may be an accurate interpretation of the last days. However, if you consider this in the context of world influences this rider on the black horse could be capitalism. Google capitalism and the first images that come up are black scales. Capitalism is all about the trading of commodities. And, the simple definition of commodities is hard assets like wheat, gold, and oil. Perhaps, the exorbitant prices for wheat give us a glimpse of the time period of this horse - have you been to the grocery store to buy a loaf of bread lately?

The fourth seal uncovers the work of a rider on a pale horse, which is identified as death; and Hades follows behind him. He was given power over a fourth of the earth to destroy through famine, through killing, through death, and even through death by animals. This pale or green rider is unique in that what he does causes Hades (Hell) to stay close by suggesting that Hell has no need to search for residents when accompanying this rider. Again, this could be a spiritual evil influence, a worldly influence or both. Consider Islam. Google Islam and the dominate color is a pale green. Muslims make up 25 percent of the world population (a fourth) and their most celebrated theme is death, they glorify killing and consider it the greatest honor to be killed while killing others. No wonder Hell follows this rider. Not much to do but open wide and receive the dead and misguided who find that immediately after killing themselves there is no great reward for murder.

The fifth seal uncovers something quite different from the first four seals. John sees the souls of people who have been martyred - killed because of the word of God and their testimony. They are calling out to God asking how long it will be before he judges and avenges their blood on the inhabitants of the earth. Interestingly, the response to them is not, "God is love, you shouldn't expect vengeance." No, they are given white robes and told to wait just a little while longer until the number of all those who are going to be martyred, like they were, is complete. The assurance that God is handling this.

The seals reveal increased destruction that is on the earth and getting worse just as Jesus said it would. Of course, with every force of evil by human flesh or satanic influence there is usually an overwhelmingly opposite force of good. No matter what time period, as long as the Holy Spirit is in the earth, in us, God's true church will fight and win over the forces of evil as long as they don't give up or lose hope. The question is not will we win but how we win.

For example, there is an under-reported phenomenon happening in the Middle East. A large majority of Muslims are abandoning Islam and becoming, yes, that's right, Christians. Every day, self-deceived, self-righteous radicals are murdering Christians and even their own people who disagree with them - doesn't sound like winning right? But wait, thousands more are turning to Christ because of it!

I have been hearing and reading reliable reports for years now about Muslims seeing visions and having dreams of Jesus and then flocking to the Christian churches. No, not the Evangelical, American churches but the churches in their own country and elsewhere. So often, especially in America, I think we forget that there are Christians in every part of the world and that the end-time revival that is often spoken of may have more to do with the persecution that leads to a surge of souls entering the kingdom of heaven and less to do with the outward evangelistic meetings that were so prevalent in America during the beginning of the 20th century. It may not look like winning in the news, but there is still joy in heaven as the martyrs take their place among their brothers and sisters and the newly redeemed get to know their Savior. In the words of early church father Tertullian, "The blood of the martyr is the seed of the church."

So the riders, or world influencers, are trying to conquer, they are warring, killing people, wreaking havoc on the economic stability of countries. There are tribulations for the Christians who are battling disillusionment because of all the events around them, plagues, famines, extreme weather, pandemics. There is fearfulness for those who have no idea what is going on in the world. The number of martyrs are increasing.

And then it happens. Suddenly. A massive earthquake, the sun turns black, the moon turns to blood, the stars appear to fall like ripe figs, and the sky seems to roll up like a scroll. From the most prominent (kings, presidents, CEOs, the rich) to the disenfranchised (the factory worker, the unemployed, the homeless, the slave), they all try to hide from the face of the one who sits on the throne and from the "wrath" of the lamb. This is what John sees when the sixth seal is opened.

When Jesus walked the earth, he talked about what events lead up to the unexpected moment when he catches away those who have been faithfully waiting for his return; and they are strikingly similar to what John is seeing.

Matthew records this in chapter 24:29-31:

*"Immediately after the "tribulation" of those days **the sun will be darkened, and the moon will not give its light; the stars will fall from heaven, and the powers of the heavens will be shaken.** Then the sign of the Son of Man will appear in heaven, and then all the tribes of the earth will mourn, **and they will see the Son of Man coming on the clouds of heaven with power and great glory.** And He will send His angels with a great sound of a trumpet, and they will **gather together His elect from the four winds, from** one end of heaven to the other.*

Mark records this in chapter 13:24-27:

*But in those days, after that tribulation, **the sun will be darkened, and the moon will not give its light; the stars of heaven will fall, and the powers in the heavens will be shaken. Then they will see the Son of Man coming in the clouds with great power and glory.** And then He will send His angels, and **gather together His elect from the four winds**, from the farthest part of earth to the farthest part of heaven.*

And, Luke records this event with a little less detail in chapter 21:25-28.

And there will be signs in the sun, in the moon, and in the stars; and on the earth distress of nations, with perplexity, the sea and the waves roaring; men's hearts failing them from fear and the expectation of those things which are coming on the earth, for **the powers of the heavens will be shaken.** *Then they will see* **the Son of Man coming in a cloud with power and great glory.** *Now when these things begin to happen, look up and lift up your heads, because your redemption draws near.*

All three gospels give this account of what Jesus told his disciples would be the sign of his return and when he would gather his people together. Not the sign of the end but the sign of his return. Actually, since John wrote Revelation, technically, all four gospels describe the same event that clearly tell us under what circumstances Jesus will return to earth.

- Sun goes dark, moon turns blood red, stars fall from sky -

No other place in Revelation does this sequence of events read like the gospels - only here. And it is here that we should be encouraged. Now I don't want to get into the pre-trib, post-trib rapture debate. For those of you who don't know what this means, the basics are this. There are those who believe that before things get really bad on the earth that Jesus will come back and rescue us from "the great tribulation" so that we won't have to go through it. Then there are those who believe that the church will be victorious during this "great tribulation" and will go through it so that when Jesus returns we will be ready to rule and reign with him on the earth. For the most part, both sides do believe that Jesus is coming back and that there will be a catching away of the church - the church being those individuals who have remained faithful to obey his word and expect his return. Jesus refers to it in John 14:

Let not your heart be troubled; you believe in God, believe also in Me. In My Father's house are many mansions; if it were not so, I would have told you. **I go to prepare a place for you. And if I go** *and prepare a place for you, I will come again and receive you to Myself; that where I am, there you may be also.*

Both groups also agree with Paul's account of Jesus's return. He writes:

For this we say to you by the word of the Lord, that we who are alive and remain until the coming of the Lord will by no means precede those who are asleep. **For the Lord himself will descend from heaven with a shout, with the voice of an archangel, and with the trumpet of God. And the dead in Christ will rise first. Then we who are alive and remain shall be caught up together with them in the clouds to meet the Lord in the air.** *And thus we shall always be with the Lord. Therefore comfort one another with these words.*

Both groups typically agree on the "what." However, it's the "when" which has always been the sticking point of the debate. John says that Jesus's return will happen around, or shortly before, this catastrophic event. However, if you notice, there is tribulation before and even more severe tribulation afterwards. So, no need to disagree - there is enough tribulation to go around so that both sides can claim the win in this debate.

In the past it was hard to imagine - sun going dark, moon turning to blood, stars falling from the sky. It had to be symbolism. Not today. It is not hard at all to imagine that something eerie is already happening to the earth. I can say that there have been more unexplained happenings in the sky and on earth in the last ten years than in all the time I have been alive. We know that stars or meteors have fallen from the sky and made quite an impact. Thousands of birds have fallen from the sky and rivers have turned red like blood. Millions of fish have washed up dead on the beaches. Bees are dying off and creatures only found in the depths of the sea are coming up to the surface for no apparent reason. There's been reports of unexplained noises in the earth, unexplained flashes and more UFOs than ever showing up on radar.

There are programs like CERN that is rumored to be trying to open up spiritual dimensions, and chemicals the military is putting in the air to influence weather or block radar. The self-deceived elitist with their "Dim the Sun Project" plan to spew calcium carbonate in the stratosphere to slow what they believe is global warming. There are nuclear weapons being sold like candy, and the asteroid, Apophis, on a possible collision course with earth in 2029, we have the widely accepted transhumanism movement, animal and human DNA being mixed, weaponized viruses, super soldiers, clones, and all kinds of tomfoolery in the name of science. We got X-men and Iron man...oh, wait that's not real.

As outrageous as things are today, is it so hard to imagine that moment when some knuckle-headed ego maniacs push a button or light an experiment that shakes the earth at its core and starts a chain reaction that brings on it's slow and painful destruction? The sun going dark, the moon turning to blood, the stars falling from the sky is not hard to believe these days. And just because the scroll describes these events in great detail does not mean God is responsible for them, just that they will happen. And when they do, Jesus will shout, "ENOUGH!" And, those who don't know him will be terrified. And those who do know him will be snatched up by his angels and brought up out of the chaos. This is not yet the end of the age, this is the beginning of the earth under new management and Jesus is about to clean house.

Revelation - Chapter 7

Revelation 7:1-17 KJV:

*And after these things I saw four angels standing on the four corners of the earth, holding the four winds of the earth, that the wind should not blow on the earth, nor on the sea, nor on any tree. **2** And I saw another angel ascending from the east, having the seal of the living God: and he cried with a loud voice to the four angels, to whom it was given to hurt the earth and the sea, **3** Saying, Hurt not the earth, neither the sea, nor the trees, till we have sealed the servants of our God in their foreheads. **4** And I heard the number of them which were sealed: and there were sealed an hundred and forty and four thousand of all the tribes of the children of Israel. **5** Of the tribe of Juda were sealed twelve thousand. Of the tribe of Reuben were sealed twelve thousand. Of the tribe of Gad were sealed twelve thousand. **6** Of the tribe of Aser were sealed twelve thousand. Of the tribe of Nephthalim were sealed twelve thousand. Of the tribe of Manasses were sealed twelve thousand. **7** Of the tribe of Simeon were sealed twelve thousand. Of the tribe of Levi were sealed twelve thousand.*

Of the tribe of Issachar were sealed twelve thousand. **8** *Of the tribe of Zabulon were sealed twelve thousand. Of the tribe of Joseph were sealed twelve thousand. Of the tribe of Benjamin were sealed twelve thousand.* **9** *After this I beheld, and, lo, a great multitude, which no man could number, of all nations, and kindreds, and people, and tongues, stood before the throne, and before the Lamb, clothed with white robes, and palms in their hands;* **10** *And cried with a loud voice, saying, Salvation to our God which sitteth upon the throne, and unto the Lamb.* **11** *And all the angels stood round about the throne, and about the elders and the four beasts, and fell before the throne on their faces, and worshipped God,* **12** *Saying, Amen: Blessing, and glory, and wisdom, and thanksgiving, and honour, and power, and might, be unto our God for ever and ever Amen.* **13** *And one of the elders answered, saying unto me, What are these which are arrayed in white robes? and whence came they?* **14** *And I said unto him, Sir, thou knowest. And he said to me, These are they which came out of great tribulation, and have washed their robes, and made them white in the blood of the Lamb.* **15** *Therefore are they before the throne of God, and serve him day and night in his temple: and he that sitteth on the throne shall dwell among them.* **16** *They shall hunger no more, neither thirst any more; neither shall the sun light on them, nor any heat.* **17** *For the Lamb which is in the midst of the throne shall feed them, and shall lead them unto living fountains of waters: and God shall wipe away all tears from their eyes.*

The next thing that John sees has troubled many a Christian for years. It's the dreaded 144,000. Not understanding what they were reading, many a pastor back in the day, who dared to preach on Revelation, made an erroneous assumption that only 144,000 would enter the kingdom of heaven. One religion even adopted this as their main theological message. The fact that nobody bothered to keep reading the chapter just shows how much we must depend on the Spirit of God to reveal things to us.

This 144,000 that John sees are Jews - in this one event - at the beginning of the end. Before anything else goes down, angels are sent to put God's seal on them. There are 12,000 from each of the twelve tribes of Israel (12 x 12,000 = 144,000). More about these 144,000 Jews in a later chapter. Once they are sealed, the scene abruptly changes and John sees a multitude of people from every nation standing in heaven. This revelation of John is not a slow moving train - it's a vision where things are happening fast, sometimes simultaneously.

So picture this: There is a catastrophic event on earth, Jesus appears in the clouds, his angels are dispatched to gather up his faithful ones, who are changed in the blink of an eye. While this is happening, other angels hold back the winds from the four corners of the earth while yet another angel (you get the point) places God's seal on the 144,000. Now shift your eyes upward from earth back to heaven. John looks up and sees a vast number of people, too many to count, from every tribe, every people, every tongue and every nation. They have just gathered around the throne room standing before the Lamb. They have on white robes, they've got palm branches in their hands and they are shouting with loud voices, "Worthy is the Lamb!" This is not some supervised religious service - this is a party! The creatures, the angels, the elders are beside themselves with joy. They are falling on their faces, they are laughing, they are crying, they are worshipping Jesus.

Who are these multitudes of people and where did they just come from all of a sudden? You guessed it, one second they were looking up at the unbelievable events in the sky from the planet earth, and in that same second, they are in the throne room and Jesus is presenting them before God. Jesus just brought his church home.

Of course John would be confused with all this celebratory noise and excitement going on. He had no concept of the church going much further than he and his fellow apostles. When Jesus was about to leave earth after his resurrection, they asked him. "Are you going to restore Jerusalem at this time? Jesus basically told them, "Don't worry about that you just wait here in Jerusalem until the Holy Spirit comes to help you. People use this verse to imply that we are not to know anything about the future. However, the book of Revelation completely destroys that argument. Think about it. How practical would it have been for Jesus to tell them, "No, not now, It's going to be approximately 1,948 years before Jerusalem will be a nation again." No, the disciples would not have been able to see that far down the road.

John's reaction is so removed, so inappropriately non-celebratory that one of the elders has to come over to him and ask, "Do you know who these people are and where they came from?" John is clueless. The elder says, "These are the ones who came out of the great tribulation." Did you hear that? The elder said these people have made it out of the great tribulation. These people of God are safely in heaven.

You might be thinking, *well I know Christians who have lived a ripe old age and died, they were never martyred or in that great tribulation of the end times, are they included in this throng of people?* Yes. Perhaps we have made "The great tribulation" a single event without fully understanding how God sees it. I have no problem at all believing this elder. After living on this earth with all its heartache and pain and suffering. I have gone through great tribulation. In fact any believer who doesn't go straight to heaven after they accept Christ has gone through great tribulation. If we believe what John saw and what the elder says then this multitude is all of us who will no longer have to hunger and thirst for righteousness again. God has wiped away every one of our tears and we belong to Jesus. Is there more tribulation to come? Absolutely, but not for the people of God who were watching and waiting for his return.

What of the 144,000? We will see later in Revelation that they are also safe with Jesus. They were marked with the Holy Spirit's seal, or tagged, as being purchased with the blood of Jesus, just like the rest of us who believe. Here's what the scripture says about those who are marked. Ephesians 1:13-14, *"And because of what Christ did, all you others too, who heard the Good News about how to be saved, and trusted Christ, were marked as belonging to Christ by the Holy Spirit, who long ago had been promised to all of us Christians. His presence within us is God's guarantee that he really will give us all that he promised; and **the Spirit's seal upon us means that God has already purchased us and that he guarantees to bring us to himself**. This is just one more reason for us to praise our glorious God."*

If you are not familiar with how the Jewish race fits into Revelation, just know that the whole of the Bible, including Revelation, is a family affair about the Jews and how we Gentiles fit into that family. It all started with Abraham. He was a man who believed God when few people in his day did. God told him that because he believed and obeyed him, he would bless him and give him and his wife Sarah a son. God said Abraham's seed would eventually cause all the nations on the earth to be blessed. Since Abraham was old and his wife was barren, they came up with an alternative plan - a surrogate mother. Unfortunately, Abraham's plan B continues to cause much conflict. The child of Abraham and Sarah's slave, Ishmael, became the Arab race. God did bless Ishmael but God gave Abraham and Sarah the ability to have a son in their old age; and this promised son Isaac then had a son, Jacob. Jacob (who's name was later changed to Israel by God) had 12 sons, who then had sons, and so on. That family is the Jewish race, the twelve tribes of Israel are the twelve sons of Jacob. Jews are Abraham's kids. Unfortunately, they rejected God's plan to save the whole world. When Jesus (Abraham's seed that would cause all nations of the earth to be blessed) came the first time, the Jews rejected him as their Messiah (something God knew they would do). As a result, we Gentiles (everyone else) have been given the opportunity to become members of God's family. Apostle Paul explains the circumstances surrounding Jew and Gentile in Romans 11. Here are a few excerpts from that chapter:

> ...I ask then, has God rejected and deserted his people the Jews? Oh no, not at all. Remember that I myself am a Jew, a descendant of Abraham and a member of Benjamin's family. No, God has not discarded his own people whom he chose from the very beginning.
> ...Not all the Jews have turned away from God; there are a few being saved as a result of God's kindness in choosing them. And if it is by God's kindness, then it is

not by their being good enough. For in that case the free gift would no longer be free—it isn't free when it is earned.

...So this is the situation: Most of the Jews have not found the favor of God they are looking for. A few have—the ones God has picked out—but the eyes of the others have been blinded.

...Does this mean that God has rejected his Jewish people forever? Of course not! ***His purpose was to make his salvation available to the Gentiles, and then the Jews would be jealous and begin to want God's salvation for themselves.*** *Now if the whole world became rich as a result of God's offer of salvation, when the Jews stumbled over it and turned it down, think how much greater a blessing the world will share in later on when the Jews, too, come to Christ.*

It's interesting to note that when Jesus walked the earth, it wasn't the whole of the Jewish people who rejected him. The crowds followed him and loved the miracles he did. It was the leaders who had a problem with Jesus. They were so confident in their own knowledge of the coming Messiah that they dismissed him when he tried to tell them who he was. It was political, they were afraid they would lose their power and influence over the people so they tried to destroy him with slanderous claims. And the multitudes were deceived because they let those political, religious leaders tell them what to believe instead of thinking for themselves.

It is happening again. One of the most famous Jewish Rabbis, Yitzhak Kaduri (the Billy Graham for Jews), left a note with his students to be opened one year after his death. The note was to reveal the Messiah, whom Rabbi Kaduri said had visited him in a vision. One year after his death (2007) the note revealed that Jesus was the Messiah.

The Orthodox Jews in the 21st century who are still waiting for Messiah to come, have picked up where the Pharisees from Jesus's day left off. They have been doing everything they can to discredit this note and silence those who are speaking out about its authenticity. They are, once again, afraid of losing their power and influence over the people. And the Jewish people, once again have an opportunity to think for themselves or let the political, religious leaders tell them what to believe.

God will judge all leaders (Jews or Gentiles) who lead with deceit or evil motives and intentions. But God will also judge every person who blindly follows the culture and world system of their day instead of believing what they know in their heart is true. So a nation is judged by what the leadership convinces their people to do - good or bad.

Revelation - Chapter 8

Revelation 8:1-13 KJV:

And when he had opened the seventh seal, there was silence in heaven about the space of half an hour. 2 And I saw the seven angels which stood before God; and to them were given seven trumpets. 3 And another angel came and stood at the altar, having a golden censer; and there was given unto him much incense, that he should offer it with the prayers of all saints upon the golden altar which was before the throne. 4 And the smoke of the incense, which came with the prayers of the saints, ascended up before God out of the angel's hand. 5 And the angel took the censer, and filled it with fire of the altar, and cast it into the earth: and there were voices, and thunderings, and lightnings, and an earthquake. 6 And the seven angels which had the seven trumpets prepared themselves to sound. 7 The first angel sounded, and there followed hail and fire mingled with blood, and they were cast upon the earth: and the third part of trees was burnt up, and all green grass was burnt up. 8 And the second angel sounded, and as it were a great mountain burning with fire was cast into the sea: and the third part of the sea became blood; 9 And the third part of the creatures which were in the sea, and had life, died; and the third part of the ships were destroyed. 10 And the third angel sounded, and there fell a great star from heaven, burning as it were a lamp, and it fell upon the third part of the rivers, and upon the fountains of waters; 11 And the name of the star is called Wormwood: and the third part of the waters became wormwood; and many men died of the waters, because they were made bitter. 12 And the fourth angel sounded, and the third part of the sun was smitten, and the third part of the moon, and the third part of the stars; so as the third part of them was darkened, and the day shone not for a third part of it, and the night likewise. 13 And I beheld, and heard an angel flying through the midst of heaven, saying with a loud voice, Woe, woe, woe, to the inhabiters of the earth by reason of the other voices of the trumpet of the three angels, which are yet to sound!

When Jesus opened the seventh and last seal, there was silence in heaven for half an hour. It doesn't explain why. Perhaps what was revealed was so sobering that it was necessary for Jesus to pause and take it in. And, if everyone around the throne was taking their cue from Jesus, of course, they would make no sound until he did.

The seventh and last seal reveals the final judgment of God and the wrath of the Lamb. Interesting choice of words John uses - "Wrath of the Lamb." Those two words - "wrath" and "lamb" are not typically seen together. The implication is that it was not some dictatorial, controlling deity that demanded worship who came to earth. No, God came to us as humbly

and gently as possible so that we would not be afraid to trust
him. He did everything he could do, including dying in our
place, so that we would not have to face the judgment that was
pronounced on humankind after Adam sinned.

Now it was here. And, it was going to be horrible. The
trial and the verdict had already been decided thousands of
years earlier but this was the beginning of the sentencing for
humankind. Even what was about to happen on the earth was
full of the mercy of God. When you create something and it
doesn't work as you intended, you have every right to destroy it
and throw it in the trash. God created humankind that refused
to work as it was intended but instead of destroying humankind,
he saved us from destruction. Then he did something so
remarkable it is hard to believe. He adopted his created beings
and gave us all the rights and privileges as if we were his own
children. So not only are we saved from destruction, we are
now God's heirs with all the benefits of sonship.

But not everybody believed him. In fact, according to
scripture, most rejected his help and many persecuted and killed
his heirs who were messengers of his good news. Now those
who rejected salvation, through Christ, will end up facing his
wrath. The full measure of that wrath is about to begin with
seven trumpets.

There is an assembly of seven angels, each with a trumpet,
in front of the altar of God. Incense is taken from this altar
and mixed in a golden censer (or a bowl) **with the prayers of
the people of God**. Here, the angel is enacting the equivalent
practice of burnt offerings in Jewish culture. The priest would
take live coals and drop them onto the incense, which would
fill the room with fragrance and smoke. The smoke from
this mixture rises up out of the bowl before God and elicits

51

a response. Our prayers have great significance and will always elicit a response from God, either in our present situation or at the end of the age.

I remember reading the testimony of a man who clinically died and found himself being pulled upward towards heaven by two angels. He said that he was traveling at an amazing rate of speed but that there were flashes going so fast past him towards heaven that they were a blur. The angels told him that those flashes were prayers of God's people going to heaven. Our prayers for family, for friends, for our country, prayers for God to avenge us, prayers for his kingdom to come arrive at God's throne faster than the speed of light. The scripture says, *"For the eyes of the Lord are on the righteous, and His ears are open to their prayers; But the face of the Lord is against those who do evil."*

These bowls are mentioned earlier in Revelation 5, under completely different circumstances. *"Now when He had taken the scroll, the four living creatures and the twenty-four elders fell down before the Lamb, each having a harp, and **golden bowls full of incense, which are the prayers of the saints**. And they sang a new song..."*

Apparently, these golden bowls full of prayers were an integral part of Jesus's ceremony, as he received the scroll. Perhaps it is important that we know that while Jesus died for the whole of humankind, he was very much aware of us as individuals. Just as we keep and cherish what is precious to us, God keeps every prayer we've ever prayed. Now it seems he is about to answer those prayers reserved for this particular hour. I can't help but think that these prayers are the ones which pertain to injustice. Prayers from those who were disenfranchised, marginalized, and taken advantage of on earth. Perhaps the prayers of the Martyrs that were waiting for their time of God's vengeance. Why do I think that these prayers pertain to injustice? Because of what they do to the earth. The angel adds fire from the altar to the bowl that had just been filled with incense and hurls this mixture down upon the inhabitants of the earth. This looks very much like God avenging his people. And, for those who insist that the church goes through the wrath that is coming on the earth, can you see how uncharacteristic that would be? We prayed to God and God answered our prayers by filling bowls with them and hurling them down upon us.

The seven angels begin their trumpet sounds and, with no indication of how long each event takes place or how quickly the trumpets are blown in succession, we begin the destruction of earth.

- The first trumpet: hail and fire mingled with blood hurled down to earth and a third of the trees and grass are burned up.
- The second trumpet: A great mountain burning with fire (possibly a huge volcano) is thrown into the sea and a third of the sea becomes blood along with a third of the living creatures in the sea dying and a third of the ships destroyed.
- The third trumpet: A great star falls from heaven burning like a torch and falls on a third of the rivers and springs and many die from the water.
- The fourth trumpet: A third of the sun, moon and stars are struck and darkened so that day looks like night.

Some end-time scholars suggest that the sequence of events resemble what would happen if an asteroid struck earth. An asteroid would break off as it enters the earth's atmosphere and fiery debris would rain down, then the mountains would burn and fall into the sea. Next, the actual asteroid or "star" would probably land into water and cause all the rivers and springs to cook what is in the water. Finally, this large asteroid could strike the sun, and moon and some of the stars (a third according to John's account) on its way in.

It is here that things began to get even worse. Chapter 8 ends with a further warning from an angel flying through the midst of heaven, *"Woe, woe, woe to the inhabitants of the earth, because of the remaining blasts of the trumpet of the three angels who are about to sound."*

Revelation - Chapter 9

Revelation 9:1-21 KJV:

And the fifth angel sounded, and I saw a star fall from heaven unto the earth: and to him was given the key of the bottomless pit. 2 And he opened the bottomless pit; and there arose a smoke out of the pit, as the smoke of a great furnace; and the sun and the air were darkened by reason of the smoke of the pit. 3 And there came out of the smoke locusts upon the earth: and unto them was given power, as the scorpions of the earth have power. 4 And it was commanded them that they should not hurt the grass of the earth, neither any green thing, neither any tree; but only those men which have not the seal of God in their foreheads. 5 And to them it was given that they should not kill them, but that they should be tormented five months: and their torment was as the torment of a scorpion, when he striketh a man. 6 And in those days shall men seek death, and shall not find it; and shall desire to die, and death shall flee from them. 7 And the shapes of the locusts were like unto horses prepared unto battle; and on their heads were as it were crowns like gold, and their faces were as the faces of men. 8 And they had hair as the hair of women, and their teeth were as the teeth of lions. 9 And they had breastplates, as it were breastplates of iron; and the sound of their wings was as the sound of chariots of many horses running to battle. 10 And they had tails like unto scorpions, and there were stings in their tails: and their power was to hurt men five months. 11 And they had a king over them, which is the angel of the bottomless pit, whose name in the Hebrew tongue is Abaddon, but in the Greek tongue hath his name Apollyon. 12 One woe is past; and, behold, there come two woes more hereafter. 13 And the sixth angel sounded, and I heard a voice from the four horns of the golden altar which is before God, 14 Saying to the sixth angel which had the trumpet, Loose the four angels which are bound in the great river Euphrates. 15 And the four angels were loosed, which were prepared for an hour, and a day, and a month, and a year, for to slay the third part of men. 16 And the number of the army of the horsemen were two hundred thousand thousand: and I heard the number of them. 17 And thus I saw the horses in the vision, and them that sat on them, having breastplates of fire, and of jacinth, and brimstone: and the heads of the horses were as the heads of lions; and out of their mouths issued fire and smoke and brimstone. 18 By these three was the third part of men killed, by the fire, and by the smoke, and by the brimstone, which issued out of their mouths. 19 For their power is in their mouth, and in their tails: for their tails were like unto serpents, and had heads, and with them they do hurt. 20 And the rest of the men which were not killed by these plagues yet repented not

of the works of their hands, that they should not worship
devils, and idols of gold, and silver, and brass, and stone,
and of wood: which neither can see, nor hear, nor walk:
21 Neither repented they of their murders, nor of their
sorceries, nor of their fornication, nor of their thefts.

The fifth trumpet reveals something that has not been considered in this writing until now. This star that falls from
heaven to earth is personified. *"He was given the key to the*
bottomless pit." Should we then assume that the stars in the
sky are actually living, conscious-minded beings? Why not?
The truth is everything that God made is living and active. It is
not too far-fetched to believe that the stars are possibly angels.
Jesus, himself, has been described as being brighter than the sun
with eyes like flames of fire. Angels are always seen as lights.
Even satan has been described as a deceiving "angel of light" by
Paul. Angels, as stars on assignment, actually give much clarity
to what we read in the scriptures. God says in Isaiah that he
can command the stars to appear to him in order. According
to Genesis, angels are still at their post guarding the tree of life
in the Garden of Eden, for over six thousand years now. It was
a bright star in the east that was guiding the wise men to Jesus.
How do you make a star shine brighter on a certain year, month,
or day? You tell it to. God told this star when and how to shine.
The shepherds in the field looked up and saw a host of angels
praising God because Jesus was born. They could have traveled
from heaven to earth faster than the speed of light or perhaps
they were already there, doing what they were assigned to do -
shining over this tiny planet earth.

Whether you believe stars in the sky are balls of gas or angels, it doesn't really matter. Everything in heaven, earth and under the earth responds to God's word. Rocks would cry out, Jesus told the Pharisees, if the people weren't able to praise him. The wind died down when Jesus rebuked it, the oceans only come onto the land so far, because God tells it to, according to the book of Job. The only thing that believing that stars are angels does is make further sense of the scenarios we have been reading. The star (angel) left his post in the heavens and took the key he was given to open the bottomless pit.

What's in the bottomless pit? More trouble for those left on the earth who do not have the seal of God on their forehead. John does not tell us, perhaps he doesn't know, whether what comes out of the bottomless pit is visible or invisible to the inhabitants of the earth. But let's assume for the moment that what he sees will be visible.

The bottomless pit is open and the smoke from this pit is so overpowering that it darkens the already darkened sun. But wait, it isn't just smoke that darkens the sun, it's locusts! And, not your run-of-the-mill terrifying swarm of locusts from the stories told by farmers. No, these are bottomless pit locusts.

John says, *"The locusts looked like horses armored for battle. They had what looked like golden crowns on their heads, and their faces looked like men's. Their hair was long like a woman, and their teeth were those of lions. They wore breastplates that seemed to be of iron, and their wings roared like an army of chariots rushing into battle."*

They were given the most fantastical restriction. Do not touch the grass, or any tree, or any green thing. Wait, isn't that what locust eat when they swarm in? They kill the green vegetation by eating it all. But these locusts are commanded not to do it. So what do they do? They terrorize humankind for five months.

58

Ive heard some say that these locusts John sees could actually be drones sent to regain control of civil chaos because of the events happening in the world. That is very possible. I would imagine that it would take five months to get back to some form of normalcy after the unbelievable goings on. There are other very possible theories of what John just saw.

There was a story of a young boy in Mexico City who found a very eerie-looking, demon-like creature along a trail near his home. It had wings, a face, hair, teeth and a tail that looked like it had a stinger on the end. The village people called it a fairy and at least one person indicated that they had seen one alive. This one had been shot down with what appeared to be buck shots. Seeing this thing on a computer screen was a little eerie, seeing it alive would be scary, but seeing millions of them would be terrifying. Those radicals out there killing and beheading people think they've cornered the market on terror. You don't know "nothin' bout terror" till you see a swarm of a million demon-looking locusts not trying to go after the vegetation but using their scorpion-like stingers to go after *you*!

This happened before. Look at Exodus 8, Pharaoh and the people of Egypt not only saw locusts but frogs, flies, and lice coming on them at God's command through Moses. But demon-looking creatures with hair, and faces, and teeth, and wings, that sounds like a hoax. What was found could have been a hoax, but lately there have been creatures mysteriously washing up on shore that look just as freakishly horrifying as this locust John described.

Another scenario would be if these locusts are not visible. Their stingers could bring on a physical malady to the people of earth. Consider something like the vaccines that are even now causing unexplainable side affects. Perhaps a future vaccine that

59

citizens will have to take, or else. Who would have believed that a time would come when democratic systems of government would be forcing its citizens to comply with whatever greed-motivated big tech and big pharma recommend. Sweden is already using microchips on their citizens today. Some are reporting, at their own risk, that the technology used in vaccines and microchips can be programmed to administer relief, pain or even death. Is the technology to do this already here and being used on unwitting subjects?

The next woe for the earth is when the sixth angel sounds his trumpet and four angels, bound in the great Euphrates river, are released. John says they have been kept ready for this day and hour. They have with them an army of 200 million demons with tails like snakes; and fire, smoke and sulfur coming out of their mouth

Opening up a prison cell with a powerful fallen angel inside and his millions of swarms of locusts that can sting like scorpions, and then releasing angels bound at the bottom of the Euphrates river with an army of 200 million demons, sounds like a fight is being organized - and humankind is caught in the middle. These powerful evil beings unleash their stored up fury on the inhabitants of the earth. The demon looking locusts only terrorize for five months. However, the army from the Euphrates river actually kills a third of humankind.

We are told by John that the inhabitants on the earth continue to worship demons, and idols, and silver, and gold. They are still murdering and practicing witchcraft and refuse to repent of their sorcery, immorality, or their thievery. If the locusts and the demon army are not visible but the result of their terror looks like people dying from military war or from physical reactions to a virus, this might explain why things seem to be business as usual, with people continuing demon and idol worship, and trying to get rich. Surely, if these things were visible, the inhabitants of earth would be too preoccupied with the terror of it all to be trying to get rich.

Why are the inhabitants on the earth just continuing to sin and practice witchcraft? Why is there no crying out to God for help? Well, if the events laid out here are correct, what would be their motivation to bow their heads and pray? Why would they think that God would hear them? Jesus has come back in a dramatic demonstration in the sky, the earth is convulsing and falling apart everywhere. The true church, along with every child in and out of the womb has been taken from earth. The people who didn't really believe in Christ, but pretended to, are left with only themselves to blame. The Holy Spirit is no longer on the earth, which means there is no longer peace on the earth. The lawlessness and killing is over the top - what is there to restrain the demonic activity? Who can stop them from wreaking havoc? The hopelessness, despair, and fear would be unimaginable. My theology tells me that God hears a sincere prayer no matter the conditions; as long as one believes that he exists and that he will answer. In other words, as long as they come to him in faith. Unfortunately, the amount of spiritual strength it would take to muster up a sincere prayer of faith under these tremendously difficult circumstances is almost impossible. We are truly living in a time of grace. And unfortunately, most won't realize it until it's gone.

There is evidence in Revelation that some do believe after Jesus has collected his church. Perhaps this is why these events continue to go on for many more chapters. As long as there is a remnant who believe, God will always be there to rescue them, even if only a handful. But we should not be foolishly flippant about the "day after." I've heard those who say, "Well, if the rapture happens, then I will believe in Jesus." And, I say, if you had the kind of faith to stand up against all the natural and supernatural terror and chaos that comes after we leave, then you would have already been able to stand up to the puny peer pressure and inconveniences that stop you from becoming a Christian today. And if you are intimidated about being labeled a Christian today, you won't have near enough courage to become a Christian then, when your physical life is threatened.

Revelation - Chapter 10

Revelation 10:1-11 KJV:

And I saw another mighty angel come down from heaven, clothed with a cloud: and a rainbow was upon his head, and his face was as it were the sun, and his feet as pillars of fire: 2 And he had in his hand a little book open: and he set his right foot upon the sea, and his left foot on the earth, 3 And cried with a loud voice, as when a lion roareth: and when he had cried, seven thunders uttered their voices. 4 And when the seven thunders had uttered their voices, I was about to write: and I heard a voice from heaven saying unto me, Seal up those things which the seven thunders uttered, and write them not. 5 And the angel which I saw stand upon the sea and upon the earth lifted up his hand to heaven, 6 And sware by him that liveth for ever and ever, who created heaven, and the things that therein are, and the earth, and the things that therein are, and the sea, and the things which are therein, that there should be time no longer: 7 But in the days of the voice of the seventh angel, when he shall begin to sound, the mystery of God should be finished, as he hath declared to his servants the prophets.

8 And the voice which I heard from heaven spake unto me again, and said, Go and take the little book which is open in the hand of the angel which standeth upon the sea and upon the earth. 9 And I went unto the angel, and said unto him, Give me the little book. And he said unto me, Take it, and eat it up; and it shall make thy belly bitter, but it shall be in thy mouth sweet as honey. 10 And I took the little book out of the angel's hand, and ate it up; and it was in my mouth sweet as honey: and as soon as I had eaten it, my belly was bitter. 11 And he said unto me, Thou must prophesy again before many peoples, and nations, and tongues, and kings.

John now sees a huge, mighty angel coming down from heaven surrounded by a cloud with a whole rainbow over his head. He's got one foot on the sea and the other foot on the earth and he starts shouting but it sounds like the roar of a lion. Can you just imagine what John is seeing? It probably took him months to recover from the magnitude of it all.

Although, the interaction between the natural and the supernatural was not strange to John. In the three years he was his disciple, John saw Jesus cast out demons from a myriad of people. He saw Jesus rebuke and calm what looked like a category 5 hurricane that threatened to topple the boat they were in. He saw Jesus in his glorified body on the mountain of transfiguration. And, he heard the voice of God speak audibly out of the clouds. John had seen some pretty remarkable things walking with Jesus. But what he was seeing this day was far more extraordinary. The future state of the world was overwhelmingly evil. Sin increased, angelic and demonic activity increased and the turmoil of the earth increased. Jesus said as it was in the days of Noah, so it will be at the end of the age. (Luke 17:26).

What was it like in the days of Noah? It was bad. From the time that Adam first disobeyed God until the time of Noah was approximately 1600 years. And in that time, just as God said, humankind became more and more evil and more and more attracted to evil than to God. Genesis 6:4-7 says, *In those days, **and even afterwards**, when the evil beings from the spirit world were sexually involved with human women, their children became giants, of whom so many legends are told. When the Lord God saw the extent of human wickedness, and that the trend and direction of men's lives were only towards evil, he was sorry he had made them. It broke his heart. And he said, "I will blot out from the face of the earth all mankind that I created. Yes, and the animals too, and the reptiles and the birds. For I am sorry I made them." But Noah was a pleasure to the Lord.*

The most obvious telltale sign of the days of Noah according to this passage was that humankind departed from the natural order that God designed for them and that their bend was always towards evil. It is not a stretch to see that happening today. However, there was a bright spot in God's heart - his name was Noah. Why was Noah a pleasure to the Lord? The same reason Abraham was, and David was, and anyone who believes that God is good and values a relationship with him. The scriptures say of Noah:*"He was the only truly righteous man living on the earth at that time. He tried always to conduct his affairs according to God's will.... Meanwhile, the crime rate was rising rapidly across the earth, and, as seen by God, the world was rotten to the core. As God observed how bad it was, and saw that all mankind was vicious and depraved, he said to Noah, "I have decided to destroy all mankind; for the earth is filled with crime because of man. Yes, I will destroy mankind from the earth. Make a boat..."*

I have heard it said that Noah was the only one righteous because he had not defiled himself with the sexual perversion of the fallen angels so his lineage was pure. While this is probably true, consider that there may have been others who had not taken part in the wickedness and depravity all around but were not considered righteous. What if there were others who were disgusted with what was going on but who thought it was not their place to tell people what to do. What about those who laughed it off as no big deal. And those who said, "Why get so worked up about sin, Noah? God doesn't care about sin - he wants us to be happy." Or those who chimed in, "Don't judge!" They weren't righteous because they took no stand for the things of God. They were neither hot nor cold - lukewarm, I believe Jesus called them.

The invitation to enter the ark was open to anyone who believed that God did care and was grieved with what was going on. The invitation was open to anyone who didn't think it was cool to be dabbling with spiritual wickedness. The invitation was open to anyone who was not more concerned about offending their culture or social norms than of offending God. The invitation was open - that is until it started to rain. By then, it was too late. Anyone trying to get into the ark at this point was not taking a stand for God or truth or righteousness. Anyone trying to get into the ark after the rain started was just trying to save their own life. And that's not righteousness. So, if what you are doing or saying on social media or in the pulpit or among your unsaved friends is more about you preserving your own life and reputation than taking a stand for God, then you are not righteous, just foolish because you know the truth but don't stand on the side of it.

As in the days of Noah, so shall it be at the end of the age. In Revelation, it is now the end of the age and the cup of God's wrath is full. This mighty angel that John sees standing with his feet on the sea and the earth seems ready for battle. He tells John it's about to be on - no more delay. As soon as the seventh angel blows his horn, everything is going to be revealed.

This angel has a "small" scroll in his hand (there's that scroll again) and a voice from heaven tells John to take it and eat it. It tastes like honey at first but then makes his stomach bitter. Now I'm convinced that the scroll is earth's history - started out sweet, ended up bitter. Perhaps God is giving John a taste of what he has experienced with humankind. Seeing and hearing is one thing but tasting and experiencing is another. Jesus tells John you must tell what you have seen and heard. And, just so you won't forget a single thing, eat the scroll which contains all the events of the future. John is told to consume this information so that he is prepared to tell it to everyone.

Revelation - Chapter 11

And there was given me a reed like unto a rod: and the angel stood, saying, Rise, and measure the temple of God, and the altar, and them that worship therein. *2 But the court which is without the temple leave out, and measure it not; for it is given unto the Gentiles: and the holy city shall they tread under foot forty and two months. 3 And I will give power unto my two witnesses, and they shall prophesy a thousand two hundred and threescore days, clothed in sackcloth. 4 These are the two olive trees, and the two candlesticks standing before the God of the earth. 5 And if any man will hurt them, fire proceedeth out of their mouth, and devoureth their enemies: and if any man will hurt them, he must in this manner be killed. 6 These have power to shut heaven, that it rain not in the days of their prophecy: and have power over waters to turn them to blood, and to smite the earth with all plagues, as often as they will. 7 And when they shall have finished their testimony, the beast that ascendeth out of the bottomless pit shall make war against them, and shall overcome them, and kill them. 8 And their dead bodies shall lie in the street of the great city, which spiritually is called Sodom and Egypt, where also our Lord was crucified. 9 And they of the people and kindreds and tongues and nations shall see their dead bodies three days and an half, and shall not suffer their dead bodies to be put in graves. 10 And they that dwell upon the earth shall rejoice over them, and make merry, and shall send gifts one to another; because these two prophets tormented them that dwelt on the earth. 11 And after three days and an half the spirit of life from God entered into them, and they stood upon their feet; and great fear fell upon them which saw them. 12 And they heard a great voice from heaven saying unto them, Come up hither. And they ascended up to heaven in a cloud; and their enemies beheld them. 13 And the same hour was there a great earthquake, and the tenth part of the city fell, and in the earthquake were slain of men seven thousand: and the remnant were affrighted, and gave glory to the God of heaven. 14 The second woe is past; and, behold, the third woe cometh quickly. 15 And the seventh angel sounded; and there were great voices in heaven, saying, The kingdoms of this world are become the kingdoms of our Lord, and of his Christ; and he shall reign for ever and ever. 16 And the four and twenty elders, which sat before God on their seats, fell upon their faces, and worshipped God, 17 Saying, We give thee thanks, O Lord God Almighty, which art, and wast, and art to come; because thou hast taken to thee thy great power, and hast reigned. 18 And the nations were angry, and thy wrath is come, and the time of the dead, that they should be judged, and that thou shouldest give reward unto thy servants the prophets, and to the saints, and them that fear thy name, small and great; and shouldest destroy them which destroy the earth. 19 And the temple of God was opened in heaven, and there was seen in his temple the ark of his testament: and there were lightnings, and voices, and thunderings, and an earthquake, and great hail.*

John is now in Jerusalem. He is told to measure the temple that at this point has now been rebuilt, a sign for us to watch. King Solomon, the son of King David (yes, that David of David and Goliath) built a temple - a house for God so that his presence could dwell with men. It was destroyed and the Jewish people were taken into exile after they continued to disobey God. It was rebuilt under the guidance of Nehemiah and the Jews were allowed to return to Jerusalem but it was later destroyed again, approximately 40 years after Jesus's resurrection. The Jewish race has been scattered and homeless for centuries. It was not until 1948 that they were officially a nation again. In all that time and even up to a few years ago, no one, I mean no one was publicly talking about the possibility of a third temple being built. Yet John is looking at a temple in Jerusalem. Jesus is showing him the time of the end - before his return. So, how close are we to the return of Christ? There are several articles and youTube videos all discussing when a third temple will be built. Some predict before the year 2024.

God is always so precise in the scriptures. The angel tells John to "measure it." Truth is never approximate. It is what it is and it doesn't change like a lie does. The purpose of the specific measurements and exact months and days is to prove to those who are reading in the distant future that God is the Alpha and Omega, the beginning and the end, the first and the last, and he knows all past, present, and future events - he sees them all in a single glance. There is so much talk in the Christian news today about a third temple that no one will be surprised when a deal is finalized and Revelation will make even more sense.

The angel tells John not to bother measuring the outer court of this temple because it's been given to the Gentiles to trample on it for 42 months. The trampling of the outer court could very well be tourist - people visiting this historic site. I went to Israel in March of 2019 (It was an incredible experience) and let me tell you that tourism is alive and well. There were so many people from so many nations flocking to and trampling through what are considered Holy Sites, I can absolutely imagine that a third temple would attract a whole new level of tourism - and a whole new reason for Jews to make "aliyah" (to come back to Jerusalem).

Perhaps the Jewish people returning to a temple is what prompts two prophets, or witnesses as they are also referred to in Revelation, to take the stage. Jesus doesn't say where these prophets are but since he is talking about the temple, they could be positioned right outside. God was very involved with Solomon building the first temple. He was instrumental in getting King Cyrus to help the Jews rebuild the second temple but God never instructed the Jews to build a third temple. When Jesus rose from the dead, there was no need for a temple anymore. We became the temple of God - the Spirit of God dwells in us now. Perhaps, these witnesses are revealing the truth, sharing the Gospel of Jesus Christ and warning of the coming judgment of God? Could this be Israel's second chance? The nation that rejected Jesus the first time he was here? Could it be that the 3 ½ years that Jesus preached and prophesied is being repeated with these two prophets who preach and prophesy for 3 ½ years? The scriptures clearly tell us that after the fullness of the gentiles, the Jews' eyes will finally be opened (Romans 11:25). Perhaps, this is the revival of the Jews that we are expecting.

Who are these witnesses? They could be people living in Jerusalem today. The scripture gives us no indication of who they are or where they come from, only that they are grieved with what is going on and began prophesying as they are instructed by God.

Most believe the witnesses are Moses and Elijah because they were the two meeting with Jesus on the mount of transfiguration in Matthew 17- perhaps discussing this very event. Others believe that Enoch and Elijah are the witnesses. Why these two? The scriptures say it is appointed for man once to die and then the judgment. The scriptures say when Enoch was 365 years old, and in constant touch with God, he disappeared, for God took him so he didn't die. And, technically, Elijah has never died either. He was carried up by angels in a flaming chariot. I know, I know, it sounds laughable but only because we've been conditioned to believe that spiritual things are less real than natural things. However, God says it's the opposite. Spiritual things are more real than what we see with our eyes. 2 Corinthians 4:18 says, "...For the things which are seen *are* temporary, but the things which are not seen *are* eternal." And without the conditioning, what happened to Elijah is really no more laughable than saying men went up in a spaceship and landed on the moon.

Consider this scenario, right outside the temple there are these two guys clothed in sackcloth preaching that Jesus is their

72

Messiah and warning people of the coming judgment. These witnesses prophesy for three and a half years. And, when they do, you know they will have full news coverage along with full commentary from the media. Now, there is no mention of when they begin - they may begin preaching and prophesying as soon as the temple goes public. Prophesying in today's culture will get you unwanted negative attention. However, prophesying after Jesus has come in the clouds will get you killed. While we don't know the spiritual climate when they start, we definitely know the spiritual climate when they end. Nobody, I mean nobody wants to hear what they have to say. The words of these prophets are like nails on a chalkboard. However, they have been given supernatural power to defend themselves and to bring plagues on the earth if necessary. No one can stop them - that is until they finish their assignment. The beast from the bottomless pit (discussed later) makes war on them and they are overcome and killed.

Murder of prophets has been happening for quite some time. Someone comes out on the side of truth and satan makes war on them using human puppets to drag up and distort any event in their life that will categorize them in the most unfavorable light. It used to be subtle. However, nowadays the verbal assault is a full on character assassination. Not only is it suggested that we question everything about the person who gets targeted, now it's suggested that we do whatever it takes to physically get rid of that person who has become an enemy of the social (evil) norm. And in the end of the last days when the people of God are gone, no truth will be tolerated.

Daniel chapter 12 refers to the end time climate. The angel tells Daniel, *"And there shall be a time of trouble, such as never was since there was a nation, even to that time. **And at that time your***

people shall be delivered, everyone who is found written in the
book. And many of those who sleep in the dust of the earth shall
awake..."*...But you, Daniel, shut up the words, and seal the book*
until the time of the end" Daniel presses the issue, "How long will
it be?" He has seen some remarkable things and is even more
puzzled. The angel tells him the last three and a half years will
be the ultimate decline. *"...and when the power of the holy people*
has been completely shattered, all these things shall be finished."

The power of the last holy people on earth is about to be
shattered. These witnesses are not just slandered but killed,
and the world rejoices. This is a global event. Everyone is so
happy that these nuisances that have been on the news for years
are dead. Nobody even cares that the officials leave their bodies
in the street. In fact officials from other countries send gifts to
Israel to celebrate. I can just see the news reports, "The Two
So-Called Prophets of God are dead!"

However, after laying dead in the street for three and a half
days, God publicly raises them up and commands them to come
up to him where they ascend to heaven in a cloud - a second
or mini rapture. At the very moment the witnesses rise up, the
city falls down. There is another massive earthquake that kills
a tenth of the city - 7,000 people, and the survivors who are
completely terrified give glory to the God of heaven. Notice
the same scenario as the first gathering. People of God go up -
massive earthquake comes down.

Now the seventh trumpet sounds. Listen to what John hears
in heaven: *"The kingdoms of the world has become the kingdoms*
of our Lord and of his Messiah, and he will reign for ever and ever."
They declare: *"... **The time has come for judging the dead, and***
for rewarding your servants the prophets and your people who
revere your name, both great and small—and for destroying

those who destroy the earth."

God's temple is opened in heaven. And within the temple, there is the Ark of the Covenant! (Moses built an exact replica of it on earth). There was a man who said he found it back in 1996. No one believed him because he seemed a little wackadoo (probably because he said he found it). He said it was in Israel buried under what would have been Golgotha - the place where Jesus was crucified. That would mean the blood of Jesus that was spilled, when he was crucified, would have seeped down through the ground and possibly dropped on the mercy seat of the Ark of the Covenant. It would be just like God to have done this. And, though he said he reported his findings to the Jewish leaders, they deny all his claims. However, the replica really does exist as does the real one in heaven. When John sees the Ark of the Covenant in heaven, there is a dramatic display of lightning and thunder, hailstorm and another massive earthquake coming on the earth.

And this, my friends, is the main narrative of Revelation. I believe that chapters 1-11, half the book, is John being shown the beginning of the last days to the beginning of the final judgment. The rest of Revelation is John seeing the retelling of some of the story with highlights about the spiritual implications of what was happening in the natural world. We learn more about satan's history, Israel's history, and the future wrath of God poured out on the earth. We see what would have happened to all of us if it had not been for Jesus, our Lord and Messiah. Fortunately, anyone whose name is written in the Lamb's Book of Life will not have to fear the judgments of God to come. Is your name written in his book?

Revelation - Chapter 12

Revelation 12:1-17 KJV:

And there appeared a great wonder in heaven; a woman clothed with the sun, and the moon under her feet, and upon her head a crown of twelve stars: 2 And she being with child cried, travailing in birth, and pained to be delivered. 3 And there appeared another wonder in heaven; and behold a great red dragon, having seven heads and ten horns, and seven crowns upon his heads. 4 And his tail drew the third part of the stars of heaven, and did cast them to the earth: and the dragon stood before the woman which was ready to be delivered, for to devour her child as soon as it was born. 5 And she brought forth a man child, who was to rule all nations with a rod of iron: and her child was caught up unto God, and to his throne. 6 And the woman fled into the wilderness, where she hath a place prepared of God, that they should feed her there a thousand two hundred and threescore days. 7 And there was war in heaven: Michael and his angels fought against the dragon; and the dragon fought and his angels, 8 And prevailed not; neither was their place found any more in heaven. 9

And the great dragon was cast out, that old serpent, called the Devil, and Satan, which deceiveth the whole world: he was cast out into the earth, and his angels were cast out with him. 10 And I heard a loud voice saying in heaven, Now is come salvation, and strength, and the kingdom of our God, and the power of his Christ: for the accuser of our brethren is cast down, which accused them before our God day and night. 11 And they overcame him by the blood of the Lamb, and by the word of their testimony; and they loved not their lives unto the death. 12 Therefore rejoice, ye heavens, and ye that dwell in them. Woe to the inhabiters of the earth and of the sea! for the devil is come down unto you, having great wrath, because he knoweth that he hath but a short time. 13 And when the dragon saw that he was cast unto the earth, he persecuted the woman which brought forth the man child. 14 And to the woman were given two wings of a great eagle, that she might fly into the wilderness, into her place, where she is nourished for a time, and times, and half a time, from the face of the serpent. 15 And the serpent cast out of his mouth water as a flood after the woman, that he might cause her to be carried away of the flood. 16 And the earth helped the woman, and the earth opened her mouth, and swallowed up the flood which the dragon cast out of his mouth. 17 And the dragon was wroth with the woman, and went to make war with the remnant of her seed, which keep the commandments of God, and have the testimony of Jesus Christ.

Chapter 12 begins with John seeing something of great significance. The Living Bible translation describes it as a pageant that took place before John's eyes. Other translations call it a portent or a harbinger - an indicator of something which the observer should pay attention. Another version translates it as a "sign," and another a "wonder." The implication is that this is different than what John has been seeing up to this point.

The pageant opens with a woman clothed with the sun, the moon under her feet and a garland of twelve stars on her head. She is pregnant and cries out in pain as she is about to give birth. This is generally accepted as a spiritual representation of Israel and the twelve stars on her head represent the twelve tribes. The child represents Christ who was birthed out of the nation of Israel when he came to earth as a baby.

Then the pageant continues with a great red dragon with seven heads, ten horns, and seven crowns on his head (these numbers will be significant as we continue reading). This dragon is symbolic of satan. Typically in a vision recorded in scripture, the heads and horns on a creature almost always represent earthly kings and kingdoms. And stars usually symbolize godly nations, people and angels. Scripture tells us that satan was responsible for a third of the angels rebelling against God and being cast down to earth. This is shown by the tail of this dragon sweeping a third of the stars out of the sky, in John's vision.

John says, *"And the dragon stood before the woman who was ready to give birth, to devour her Child as soon as it was born."* The dragon (satan) was ready to devour this child of Israel. Why? How did he know the significance of a child being born? He knew from the very beginning - in the garden. Genesis chapter 3 says the serpent was the craftiest of all the animals God made. That wasn't a bad thing until he used his craftiness against his own creator, just like satan did. And as a result, he got himself cursed. While God cursed the serpent for his act of deception, he was also sending his mentor, satan, a message. *"From now on you and the woman will be enemies, as will your offspring and hers.* **You will strike his heel, but he will crush your head.**" A child would cause satan's demise. From that time on, though satan perhaps gloated in his victory of tricking Adam into handing over the deed to earth, he was also anxiously surveilling humankind looking for any spiritual activity that surrounded a child - looking for any time that God's angels took particular interest.

Pharaoh had newborn males thrown into the Nile river. Perhaps because of the spiritual activity surrounding the birth of Moses. The evil king Herod killed all the children two years old and under after the wise men told him about the bright star (spiritual activity) shining over the newborn of Joseph and Mary. It's plausible that all throughout history satan has been wringing his hands, plotting, and planning - God's ancient words still in his ears— trying to find this child who was going to destroy him so he can destroy him first.

Long story short, it didn't work and he missed him. John sees the child caught up to God and to "his throne." The woman flees to the wilderness — 1,260, or three and a half years according to the Jewish calendar.

After this child (Jesus) is taken up, a war breaks out in heaven between satan's army and heaven's. This seems to indicate that satan was not confined to earth or in hell before Jesus was born. The scriptures are not definitive on this, but there are several passages that indicate that satan still had access to heaven, and even made frequent use of it, taking the opportunity to "accuse the brethren day and night" before God's throne. But the Bible certainly makes no mention of hell being his domain or that he is in power there. In later chapters, Revelation will make it clear what role satan will play in hell.

But this battle that John sees is specifically waged to kick satan out of heaven. The freedom he enjoyed to come and go as he pleased was over. Before, he had a right to be there - he had the deed. A deed he stole from Adam but a legitimate right nonetheless to attend the board meetings of heaven and report on the status of this planet. However, Jesus got the deed back on behalf of humankind. The first Adam failed through his disobedience. But the second Adam succeeded through his obedience. And now satan, who refused to go quietly, was permanently evicted from heaven. Michael and his angels basically said, "You ain't gotta go home but you gotta leave here!"

Can you imagine heaven having to put up with satan and his accusations against humankind day and night for ages? Poo pooing on every good report? It was a good day in heaven and a bad day on earth because that day as satan and his angels were kicked out, they came to earth angry and ready to retaliate. John sees the dragon go after Israel with a vengeance. Most people think after Jesus was crucified, it was God who went after Israel with a vengeance. However, this scripture is clear - Israel was on satan's hit list and so was everyone else who kept the commands of God.

Revelation - Chapter 13

Revelation 13:1-18 KJV:

And I stood upon the sand of the sea, and saw a beast rise up out of the sea, having seven heads and ten horns, and upon his horns ten crowns, and upon his heads the name of blasphemy. 2 And the beast which I saw was like unto a leopard, and his feet were as the feet of a bear, and his mouth as the mouth of a lion: and the dragon gave him his power, and his seat, and great authority. 3 And I saw one of his heads as it were wounded to death; and his deadly wound was healed: and all the world wondered after the beast. 4 And they worshipped the dragon which gave power unto the beast: and they worshipped the beast, saying, Who is like unto the beast? who is able to make war with him? 5 And there was given unto him a mouth speaking great things and blasphemies; and power was given unto him to continue forty and two months. 6 And he opened his mouth in blasphemy against God, to blaspheme his name, and his tabernacle, and them that dwell in heaven. 7 And it was given unto him to make war with the saints, and to overcome them: and power was given him over all kindreds, and tongues, and nations. 8 And all that dwell upon the earth shall worship him, whose names are not written in the book of life of the Lamb slain from the foundation of the world. 9 If any man have an ear, let him hear. 10 He that leadeth into captivity shall go into captivity: he that killeth with the sword must be killed with the sword. Here is the patience and the faith of the saints. 11 And I beheld another beast coming up out of the earth; and he had two horns like a lamb, and he spake as a dragon. 12 And he exerciseth all the power of the first beast before him, and causeth the earth and them which dwell therein to worship the first beast, whose deadly wound was healed. 13 And he doeth great wonders, so that he maketh fire come down from heaven on the earth in the sight of men, 14 And deceiveth them that dwell on the earth by the means of those miracles which he had power to do in the sight of the beast; saying to them that dwell on the earth, that they should make an image to the beast, which had the wound by a sword, and did live. 15 And he had power to give life unto the image of the beast, that the image of the beast should both speak, and cause that as many as would not worship the image of the beast should be killed. 16 And he causeth all, both small and great, rich and poor, free and bond, to receive a mark in their right hand, or in their foreheads: 17 And that no man might buy or sell, save he that had the mark, or the name of the beast, or the number of his name. 18 Here is wisdom. Let him that hath understanding count the number of the beast: for it is the number of a man; and his number is Six hundred threescore and six.

The pageant from chapter 12 continues and John sees a beast rising out of the water. There are some fascinating similarities in what John records in Revelation and what Daniel records in the Book of Daniel thousands of years earlier. This is significant because Daniel is also given several dreams (pageants) about the last days and the end of the age. Daniel's visions span a much longer period of time as he is shown things that will happen to his people from his generation up until the end of the age. So, for example, instead of seeing one beast rising out of the water like John did, Daniel sees four, with the fourth one being the last one. This will make more sense as I continue. Understandably, both Daniel and John are greatly disturbed by what they see. Look at the similarities between Revelation 13 and Daniel 7:

John sees a beast rising out of the sea with seven heads and ten horns; Daniel sees a fourth beast rising out of the sea and it had ten horns

John describes this beast as a leopard with feet like a bear and a mouth like a lion, Daniel says the beast is too dreadful to describe

John says the beast was given power, a throne, and great authority from the dragon; Daniel says this beast is incredibly strong and more brutal than the others

John says the dragon encouraged the beast to speak great blasphemies against God; Daniel says one of the horns on the beast had a bragging mouth and arrogant against God

John says the dragon gave the beast power to fight against God's people and overcome them; Daniel says the beast will defy God wear down the saints with persecution, try to change laws

John says all whose names were not in the Lamb's Book of Life worshipped this evil creature; Daniel says this beast will devour the whole world

Daniel is told in his vision that all the beasts he sees represent kingdoms rising out of the sea of humanity - their horns represent the kings over those kingdoms. For future reference, since the angel is showing Daniel the end times of which John is seeing, it is safe to assume that the same interpretations would apply to the beasts in Revelation. One of the heads of the beast received a fatal wound but was healed. End-time prophets believe this one head is referring to Russia. If you are old enough to remember, Russia used to be called the USSR or Soviet Union. It was dissolved in 1991. But as you can see in the news, Russia is very much alive and still trying to take over the world.

This fourth beast is the last world power before, in Daniel's words, *"... the arrival of a Man—or so he seemed to be—brought there on clouds from heaven; he approached the Ancient of Days and was presented to him. He was given the ruling power and glory over all the nations of the world, so that all people of every language must obey him. His power is eternal—it will never end; his government shall never fall."* (Daniel 7:13-14)

We don't have to guess, we know this man is Jesus. We know when he is presented before God and given authority over all the nations of the world. We just read about it in Chapter 5. The last kingdom on earth will be an eternal one. Daniel's fourth beast is eventually destroyed and stripped of his power and the angel tells Daniel that all nations and power under heaven will be given to Jesus, right? Nope, that's not what the angel says. He says all nations and power under heaven will be given to the people of God to rule forever! The people of God rescued from the horrible consequences of sin on earth, will eventually be back as the ruling power on earth under Christ's command, just as God intended from the beginning. We will not be sitting

84

around sipping milk and honey, some of us will be ruling future nations on the earth. We will discuss the role of the people of God in a later chapter.

John sees another creature; this one is coming up out of the earth. We know that these creatures represent kingdoms or empires and their horns represent kings and leaders. And, we also know that the sea they come out of represent people, we can assume that this second creature with only two horns and coming up out of the earth is a smaller leader and perhaps only represents a smaller group of people. However, this beast (also known as the false prophet) has the same authority as the first beast. How interesting that it looks like an innocent lamb but has a voice like a dragon. The implication is that it is deceiving (dragon in sheep's clothing). Its purpose is to encourage worship of the first beast and to get people to take the mark.

Let's recap, the dragon represents satan. He gives power to certain world leaders (beast with seven heads and ten horns) to carry out his agenda, which is ultimately to blaspheme God, make war with the people of God, and be worshipped. A second power (the second beast or false prophet) either starts out godly and becomes corrupt or presents itself as godly and was always corrupt. This empire is no better than the other but is able to dazzle the masses with its great miraculous power. End-time prophets say this second beast could be a religious organization like Catholicism, which seems to have a reputation of secrecy and financial influence. They are the only religious organization holding a seat in the United Nations as a member. This second beast with its two horns could also represent big tech and mainstream media since it endorses the first beast and uses its influence to encourage everyone to accept the mark of the beast. We have already seen them in action during the covid-19 pandemic. Government leaders created a scenario that required everyone to comply with big Pharma. They pushed an agenda for a desired end and the mainstream media encouraged that agenda, while successfully squelching any opposing viewpoints. Big tech made sure that if anyone disagreed with the social narrative they were removed from social media and their contracts were cancelled. Governments are becoming drunk with power. China is going to a cashless society so it can control its citizens. And you can be sure that if citizens don't comply with the whims of its government, they will be unable to buy or sell anything and eventually, if they don't take this mark, they will be killed

For many years we looked for a person, someone who would come to power and terrorize everybody into taking the mark of the beast. We expected a fantastical scenario of a leader being killed and then coming back to life making everyone on earth bow to him or her in worship (verse 3). Every world leader or president that showed the slightest inconsistency was considered the anti-Christ. Now that we are actually living in the midst of the end times the revelation of John is much clearer. We joke about getting off the grid. How data is being collected on our phones and "Alexa" and "Siri" are listening in on our conversations. Facebook and Google tracking our movements and buying habits. The anti-Christ is not some mysterious person. The anti-Christ could just be a bunch of anti-God people working for a common evil goal - to get money and power. Consider that the seven-headed, ten-horned beast is a league of nations - much like the European Union or the United Nations - whose sole purpose is to have a one-world government. There is a push to take away the autonomy of individual countries, and states, and cities. And, since sinful humans are at the head of this push, you can be sure that the fight is not for order but control as they use deception and lies woven into good causes and social justice to carry out their evil agendas. The number of this beast, 666, six being the number of man, is literally humans, humans, and humans trying to be in charge of their own destiny. Self-centered and self-absorbed puppets of satan. That foolish, prideful, ungrateful angelic being that rebelled against his creator is showing foolish, prideful, ungrateful humankind how to get themselves completely cursed just like he is.

There may be a single representative who has given over wholly to satan and his agenda. He or she may even resemble the anti-Christ often portrayed in Christian movies. However, the primary beast of Revelation does not appear to be one evil person but a combination of all kinds of ungodly leaders. If I would take a guess based on the current climate I would say that the beast includes the elite - the top one percent of the population who think they are cleverly deceiving the masses with their schemes to take over the world, it includes the elected officials who think they can do whatever they want while killing, stealing, and distorting the truth with no fear of reprisal, it includes the dictators and tyrants who force their perversions and warped ideas of leadership on their own people, and it also includes the individuals who are lovers of the world more than lovers of God. It's those who reject the truth and embrace the lie simply because of its packaging.

Revelation - Chapter 14

Revelation 14:1-20 KJV:

And I looked, and, lo, a Lamb stood on the mount Sion, and with him a hundred forty and four thousand, having his Father's name written in their foreheads. 2 And I heard a voice from heaven, as the voice of many waters, and as the voice of a great thunder: and I heard the voice of harpers harping with their harps: 3 And they sung as it were a new song before the throne, and before the four beasts, and the elders: and no man could learn that song but the hundred and forty and four thousand, which were redeemed from the earth. 4 These are they which were not defiled with women; for they are virgins. These are they which follow the Lamb whithersoever he goeth. These were redeemed from among men, being the firstfruits unto God and to the Lamb. 5 And in their mouth was found no guile: for they are without fault before the throne of God. 6 And I saw another angel fly in the midst of heaven, having the everlasting gospel to preach unto them that dwell on the earth, and to every nation, and kindred, and tongue, and people, 7 Saying with a loud voice, Fear God, and give

88

glory to him; for the hour of his judgment is come: and worship him that made heaven, and earth, and the sea, and the fountains of waters. 8 And there followed another angel, saying, Babylon is fallen, is fallen, that great city, because she made all nations drink of the wine of the wrath of her fornication. 9 And the third angel followed them, saying with a loud voice, If any man worship the beast and his image, and receive his mark in his forehead, or in his hand, 10 The same shall drink of the wine of the wrath of God, which is poured out without mixture into the cup of his indignation; and he shall be tormented with fire and brimstone in the presence of the holy angels, and in the presence of the Lamb: 11 And the smoke of their torment ascendeth up for ever and ever: and they have no rest day nor night, who worship the beast and his image, and whosoever receiveth the mark of his name. 12 Here is the patience of the saints: here are they that keep the commandments of God, and the faith of Jesus. 13 And I heard a voice from heaven saying unto me, Write, Blessed are the dead which die in the Lord from henceforth: Yea, saith the Spirit, that they may rest from their labours; and their works do follow them. 14 And I looked, and behold a white cloud, and upon the cloud one sat like unto the Son of man, having on his head a golden crown, and in his hand a sharp sickle. 15 And another angel came out of the temple, crying with a loud voice to him that sat on the cloud, Thrust in thy sickle, and reap: for the time is come for thee to reap; for the harvest of the earth is ripe. 16 And he that sat on the cloud thrust in his sickle on the earth; and the earth was reaped. 17 And another angel came out of the temple which is in heaven, he also having a sharp sickle. 18 And another angel came out from the altar, which had power over fire; and cried with a loud cry to him that had the sharp sickle, saying, Thrust in thy sharp sickle, and gather the clusters of the vine of the earth; for her grapes are fully ripe. 19 And the angel thrust in his sickle into the earth, and gathered the vine of the earth, and cast it into the great winepress of the wrath of God. 20 And the winepress was trodden without the city, and blood came out of the winepress, even unto the horse bridles, by the space of a thousand and six hundred furlongs.

Being favored can be bittersweet. It's great to be loved so much so that others take notice. But when those who take notice are jealous and full of hate, it can make your life almost unbearable. And, if God is the one who loves you and the devil is the one who hates you, it's bittersweet. Ask Job. Understand, God loves everyone, but not everyone loves God. There's nothing to be jealous about if you are witnessing a one-sided relationship - one person doing all the giving and the other person doing all the taking. It's only when two people love each other that people take notice. So satan considers greatly loved people who greatly love God a target.

What John sees next is an example of that kind of love and an elaboration of the story of the 144,000 mentioned earlier in Chapter 7. These 144,000 (12,000 from the tribes of Israel) who were marked by God as being his, are called the "firstfruits" of God's chosen people, the Jewish race. This is what Jesus wanted every Jewish person to be doing when he came the first time - keeping themselves undefiled and waiting for their Messiah.

The definition of "firstfruits" in the Bible refers to agriculture. Firstfruits was what came up first out of what you planted in the ground - and this is what was offered to the Lord in thanksgiving. It could also mean the best of the crop - usually because it did come up first. Jesus is called the firstfruits of those who have died. 1 Corinthians 15:22-24 says, *"For as in Adam all die, even so in Christ all shall be made alive. But each one in his own order: Christ the firstfruits, afterward those who are Christ's at His coming. Then comes the end..."* So, if Jesus was the firstfruits of all who would accept him when he came the first time as the sinless, spotless Lamb of God, then I can conclude that these Jews are the firstfruits of all the Jews who would accept him now that he has come as a King and a Conqueror the second time. Every eye in Israel sees Jesus when he returns. If they wouldn't accept that Jesus was the Messiah the first time he came unless he gave them a sign, well, now they have one. And though the stakes are much higher and the persecution much worse, Jews will have their opportunity to accept the kind of king they always wanted - one who came to deliver them with great power and authority.

John sees Jesus and these Jews standing with him on Mt. Zion. He also hears harps playing from heaven. This tremendous choir - 144,000 strong - sing a song before God, the living beings and the elders looking down from heaven. It's a song that nobody else could sing because no one else from the Jewish nation waited like they did.

They were not the only Jews saved or that were included in the great catching away. Jews who have recognized Jesus as the Messiah (Messianic Jews) have been entering heaven just as long as Gentiles have. But these ones who were living in the end of the last days, having no insight into the mystery that

91

God hid from them in order for us Gentiles to be saved, kept themselves undefiled by the world as they waited expectantly for their Messiah. With the push back for everything holy and set apart by the culture, they were a special group indeed.

The next thing that John sees has to do with three angels doing our job, perhaps because we are no longer there. They are preaching, prophesying, and warning. The first angel proclaims that the judgment has come and they should fear God, worship him, and give him glory. Having spent some time in a courtroom as a mediator, I had occasion to hear the instructions that attorneys would give their clients. It was important how they entered the courtroom and how they approached the judge. A flippant attitude could mean the difference between paying a little and paying a lot. This angel seems to be giving instructions to the inhabitants of earth in the same way - "When you stand before God, reverence him and give him glory."

The second angel is prophesying the doom of the great city Babylon, the city that had all the other nations eating out of her hand. There are three Chapters devoted to the fall of Babylon as John saw it. We will discuss this city when we get there.

The third angel warns the inhabitants of earth not to do it - not to worship the beast, which we defined earlier as humanity full of itself (666), attempting to be God but is being controlled by evil spirits who have evil agendas. The angel warns not to take the mark of this system on their forehead or their hands. If they do it, they will experience the full fury of God's wrath.

Why are these angels still warning people? If judgment began after the catching away of the people of God, there would be no need for warnings because all the inhabitants of earth would be doomed. Why are the angels instructed to say these things? The mercy of God is relentless. He won't stop warning until the

92

last possible moment. And the actions of these angels suggest that people will be redeemed after the church has been taken out of the earth.

Next, John hears a voice from heaven that gives us an idea of how best to get to heaven if you are one of those who missed the first opportunity. John hears a voice say, *"Write this: Blessed are the dead who die in the Lord from now on."* The voice from heaven seems to infer that since the mark of the beast is not an option, nor dying from old age, the best thing that can happen to you at this point is to be killed.

When a country's citizens find themselves away from home and there is a threat of war looming, the first thing a country's leader does is send planes or ships to take its citizens out of harm's way. Now, if you don't follow the instructions you've been given on where to be and when - if you are not ready when the ship or plane leaves, you have to get home the best way you can. Those who missed Christ's return or those who finally acknowledged Jesus as Lord in the mayhem that followed, will have to get home the old fashion way. Dying in the Lord from this moment on will be a happy ending. Personally, I want to be ready when God starts calling names to board. I don't want to be caught up in the affairs of a foreign land so much so that I'm having to dodge bullets and bombs that were never meant for me.

The next scene of this chapter seems to pick up where chapter 11 ends. Good thing too because the ending is so vague and non-descriptive, especially compared to everything else John describes. Here's how chapter 11 ends: *"Then the Temple of God in heaven was opened, and the ark of his covenant was seen inside his Temple. There were flashes of lightning, noises, peals of thunder, an earthquake, and heavy hail"* That's like reading, "The temple was opened and then a lot of stuff happened."

Well now we know what happened. John sees what comes out of the temple when it opened. Seven angels with the seven last plagues for the earth. And even though it is clear, I have to tell you, this event is explained in sort of lackluster narrative. You would think it would be presented with more dramatic flair - it's basically the climax from every major action movie you've ever seen. It's the moment that Jesus brings the final wrath of God to the earth. Clearly God doesn't get the same pleasure we get when the hero destoys the bad guy. That's because he knows and feels every hurt and every pain of every misguided, foolish human. He never wanted humankind to have to share in the punishment that was reserved for satan and the rest of the fallen angels. Again, no pleasure there either.

This climax begins with Jesus sitting on a cloud with a gold crown on his head and a sickle in his hand. He is about to avenge the death of all of the martyrs so that they will finally be at rest. Why doesn't God just forgive and forget? If you think this, then you have not known the nature of God at all. He tells us as his children to forgive those who have wronged us, not because it's not important but because he knows that we are not capable of assessing what was done to us until after we step out of our earthly bodies. Before then we would have the tendency to become bitter, or misguided in our attempt to right the wrong. But God is not blind nor deaf to the injustice done on earth. When Cain killed his brother, Abel, in a jealous rage, God heard it. Genesis 4:10 says, *"Your brother's blood calls to me from the ground. What have you done?* The implication is that the blood of a person unjustly killed cries out to God for vengeance. Perhaps this is why the final judgment is so severe. It is the culmination of all injustice from the beginning to the end. If those left on earth had repented and accepted Jesus as their savior, they would not be standing in for all humanity when Jesus returns to exact punishment. This sickle in Jesus's hand represents what the next chapter details.

Revelation - Chapter 15

Revelation 15:1-8 KJV:

And I saw another sign in heaven, great and marvellous,
seven angels having the seven last plagues; for in them
is filled up the wrath of God. *2* And I saw as it were a
sea of glass mingled with fire: and them that had gotten
the victory over the beast, and over his image, and over
his mark, and over the number of his name, stand on the
sea of glass, having the harps of God. *3* And they sing
the song of Moses the servant of God, and the song of the
Lamb, saying, Great and marvellous are thy works, Lord
God Almighty; just and true are thy ways, thou King of
saints. *4* Who shall not fear thee, O Lord, and glorify
thy name? for thou only art holy: for all nations shall
come and worship before thee; for thy judgments are made
manifest. *5* And after that I looked, and, behold, the temple
of the tabernacle of the testimony in heaven was opened:
6 And the seven angels came out of the temple, having the
seven plagues, clothed in pure and white linen, and having
their breasts girded with golden girdles. *7* And one of the
four beasts gave unto the seven angels seven golden vials

*full of the wrath of God, who liveth for ever and ever. **8**
And the temple was filled with smoke from the glory of
God, and from his power; and no man was able to enter
into the temple, till the seven plagues of the seven angels
were fulfilled.*

John sees the seven angels who are preparing to deliver the
last seven plagues. But before this happens, John sees a whole
new group of believers. It seems that the angels in chapter
14 who flew around the earth - either in the physical realm
or the spiritual realm - preaching, prophesying and warning
the people about not taking the mark were successful. By the
way, scripture says, "And this gospel of the kingdom shall be
preached in all the world for a witness unto all nations; and
then shall the end come." I've heard many a preacher say Jesus
can't come yet because we haven't reached every people group.
Don't be so sure of your calculations about how close we are to
the end. Angels can preach just like we do according to Chapter
14. While we haven't reached every people group, that will not
prevent Jesus from coming.

John describes what looks like a sea of glass and fire. Again,
a sea has represented all of humanity in previous passages in
Revelation. And fire almost always represented persecution
and refining. Standing on top of this sea are the ones who were
victorious over the beast, his image, his mark and his number.
These are those who actually made it through the worst of
the tribulation. Perhaps these are the Jews who saw Christ
return in the clouds, heard the two witnesses who prophesied,
and repented for not believing Jesus was the Messiah all along.
Perhaps these are also those who knew who Jesus was but were

not ready when he appeared. The scriptures are clear, it's not just about knowing who he is, it's about believing who he is.

Jesus gave us many examples of what his return would be like and who he was coming back for - those who were expecting him because they believed him. He told us about those who would stand before him terrified that their names were not in his book. They would tell him that they used to prophesy and do miracles in his name. But he would respond that he never knew them. Perhaps they were just attending church out of guilt or preaching and prophesying just for money. Whatever the reason, in all their religiosity, they clearly had no relationship with him. He warned about being ready when he came - not caught up in worldly affairs or getting drunk and partying.

What would happen if a woman waiting for her fiancé to return from building their dream house starts cheating on him? When he gets back he learns that instead of making plans for the wedding and anticipating his return, she has been partying with her girlfriends, going out with her exes, and dating his best friend? Do you think that this man would be okay with this relationship? Now I'm not talking about the perverted relationships that are produced in today's society; I'm talking about healthy ones with people who know the difference between right and wrong. Would they just pick up where they left off as if nothing had happened? I submit that Jesus's return is all about relationship. He is coming back for those of us who want him as much as he wants us.

These ones that John sees seem to be part of that wayward church. They weren't ready before but they have since reconciled with him. They too have a song to sing to their redeemer. With a harp in hand they sing a song of thanksgiving to the one who magnanimously rescued them. John gives us no indication of how many people there are coming out of this sea of humanity filled with persecution and fiery trials. There is no mention of a vast number or a great throng as before. And, considering the circumstances, I suppose there wouldn't be.

The seven angels are dressed in what appears to be a uniform - a spotless white robe with a gold belt across their chest. They each are handed a golden bowl by one of the living beings around the throne. These bowls are filled with the terrible wrath of God. John sees smoke from the temple and no one in heaven could enter the temple until the disbursement of the wrath of God was complete.

I recall a similar scene in the Old Testament where the smoke from the earthly temple kept anyone from entering. King Solomon had orchestrated a gathering of the priest and the singers and musicians to lavishly worship God after the temple he constructed was complete. In both cases the smoke represented the power and glory of God. What moves God to act in the Old Testament is the same thing that moves him to act in the end times. In the old, there was worship and singing and an acknowledgement that God was holy and worthy of praise by people who had humbled themselves before him. And in the new? There was worship and singing and an acknowledgement that God was holy and worthy of praise by people who had humbled themselves before him. I want to reiterate, God is provoked to wrath on the enemies of all those who worship him.

Revelation - Chapter 16

Revelation 16:1-21 KJV:

And I heard a great voice out of the temple saying to the seven angels, Go your ways, and pour out the vials of the wrath of God upon the earth. 2 And the first went, and poured out his vial upon the earth; and there fell a noisome and grievous sore upon the men which had the mark of the beast, and upon them which worshipped his image. 3 And the second angel poured out his vial upon the sea; and it became as the blood of a dead man: and every living soul died in the sea. 4 And the third angel poured out his vial upon the rivers and fountains of waters; and they became blood. 5 And I heard the angel of the waters say, Thou art righteous, O Lord, which art, and wast, and shalt be, because thou hast judged thus. 6 For they have shed the blood of saints and prophets, and thou hast given them blood to drink; for they are worthy. 7 And I heard another out of the altar say, Even so, Lord God Almighty, true and righteous are thy judgments. 8 And the fourth angel poured out his vial upon the sun; and power was given unto him to scorch men with fire. 9 And men were scorched with great heat, and blasphemed the name of God, which hath power over these plagues: and they repented not to give him glory. **10** *And the fifth angel poured out his vial upon the seat of the beast; and his kingdom was full of darkness; and they gnawed their tongues for pain,* **11** *And blasphemed the God of heaven because of their pains and their sores, and repented not of their deeds.* **12** *And the sixth angel poured out his vial upon the great river Euphrates; and the water thereof was dried up, that the way of the kings of the east might be prepared.* **13** *And I saw three unclean spirits like frogs come out of the mouth of the dragon, and out of the mouth of the beast, and out of the mouth of the false prophet.* **14** *For they are the spirits of devils, working miracles, which go forth unto the kings of the earth and of the whole world, to gather them to the battle of that great day of God Almighty.* **15** *Behold, I come as a thief. Blessed is he that watcheth, and keepeth his garments, lest he walk naked, and they see his shame.* **16** *And he gathered them together into a place called in the Hebrew tongue Armageddon.* **17** *And the seventh angel poured out his vial into the air; and there came a great voice out of the temple of heaven, from the throne, saying, It is done.* **18** *And there were voices, and thunders, and lightnings; and there was a great earthquake, such as was not since men were upon the earth, so mighty an earthquake, and so great.* **19** *And the great city was divided into three parts, and the cities of the nations fell: and great Babylon came in remembrance before God, to give unto her the cup of the wine of the fierceness of his wrath.* **20** *And every island fled away, and the mountains*

*were not found. 21 And there fell upon men a great hail
out of heaven, every stone about the weight of a talent: and
men blasphemed God because of the plague of the hail; for
the plague thereof was exceeding great.*

The voice from the temple instructs the seven angels to go and
pour out the bowls of God's wrath onto the earth. If you are
flipping through the pages and happen to start reading here,
STOP RIGHT NOW. No one should ever start at this point to
understand God. There are 15 previous chapters which show
the mercy and kindness of God. That should be your first stop.
Better yet, look at the history of humankind and then read
the Gospels - Matthew, Mark, Luke, and John. It is important
to know how we as the human race got to this point. Before
God ever pronounced judgment and poured out his wrath, he
sent warnings and poured out his mercy - in abundance. This
chapter shows us what the seven angels poured out on those
who either reluctantly or willingly took the mark of the beast,
even after all the previous warnings.

The mark of the beast has been addressed previously. Basically the beast is a system of people who try to control
everything and everyone. It is group-think, social norm, and
peer pressure. It is the number of man "6" so disgustingly full
of themselves and their ability "666" that they try to play God
in every aspect of life. Those willing to accept this foolish, self-
serving, demonically influenced system of government on their
forehead and hands will suffer the consequences. Here is a
synopsis of what happens when each bowl is poured out:

- 1. The first bowl brings gross sores on the bodies of those with the mark

- *This mark, possibly a microchip under the skin of the forehead and hand, could very well be the reason sores start breaking out on bodies.*
- 2. The second bowl poured out causes the sea to turn to blood, every living creature dies
- *The previous catastrophic events (mountains falling in the oceans, debris falling from the sky) could be the cause of every living creature dying in the waters*
- 3. The third bowl causes the rivers and springs to turn to blood
- *A chain reaction - what has transpired is now causing massive death.*
- 4. The fourth bowl is poured out and the sun is given permission to scorch the inhabitants of the earth with great heat and fire
- *In 2021, solar storms, solar flares are the latest threat to the environment. Could this be what they are experiencing?*
- 5. The fifth bowl brings darkness causing the inhabitants to gnaw their teeth in pain because of the darkness and their sores
- *A nuclear electromagnetic pulse is a burst of electromagnetic radiation created by a nuclear explosion that if used as a weapon would plunge the world into darkness and could have adverse affects on the body in the same way that 5G technology is affecting those who live around the area of the towers*
- 6. The sixth bowl causes the Euphrates river to dry up and all the rulers of the world gather for battle.
- *In 2009, the New York Times reported that the "Euphrates is drying up." No surprise that this has happened. Jesus said that the rulers of the world and their armies will gather to fight a*

final battle at Armageddon by way of the Euphrates river.
- 7. The seventh bowl is poured out and a voice from the temple in heaven says "It is finished" and Babylon is destroyed.

If you read about these judgments on the earth, and you think, as you should, that God is in control of everything and that if he didn't send the plagues, the famines, the demons, and every other horrible thing mentioned in Revelation, he surely could have stopped it, you would be right.

However, there is one very important thing you should know about God. He has never had to lift one finger to punish humankind. He's not wringing his hands and worrying about how he's going to keep control of his rebellious creation. All he did was put his words in place before the foundation of the world. Just like the law of gravity does not need to be monitored - no gravity police are necessary if you decide to step off a cliff - God's word to us on sowing and reaping does not need to be monitored. It goes like this, *"Do not be deceived, God is not mocked; for whatever a man sows, that he will also reap." (Galatians 6:7)* No need to stop men's evil plans in the last days, the more devious and diabolical they are, the more destruction they heap upon themselves both in this life and the afterlife.

Know this also about God, his nature is absolutely consistent. His grace is extraordinarily amazing, his mercy is overwhelmingly enduring, his patience has supernatural longevity, his love is exceedingly abundant...then there's his judgment - it's heart-stoppingly severe. He is kind but he is also just to the same degree. This is how God described himself to Moses as he passed in front of him, *"The Lord God, merciful and gracious, longsuffering, and abundant in goodness and truth, **keeping mercy*** *for thousands, forgiving iniquity and transgression and sin, and that will by no means clear the guilty.*

The mercy and forgiveness has been abundant, unfortunately the judgment is now overdue and this chapter ends the same way chapter 11 ends, with a few added elements, which further suggests that all that John is seeing from chapter 12 through chapter 19 are different perspectives of the final moments of earth's destruction.

Chapter 11 ends with, *"And there were noises and thunderings and lightnings; and there was a great earthquake, such a mighty and great earthquake as had not occurred since men were on the earth... "* **Chapter 16 says**, *"Then the thunder crashed and rolled, and lightning flashed; and there was a great earthquake of a magnitude unprecedented in human history."*

What two events does Chapter 16 highlight for the end of days?

- Babylon The Great receives the fierceness of God's wrath. It is destroyed and split in three sections
- The battle of Armageddon is when the armies of the world gather against Israel and against God, near a mountain area in Israel called Megiddo, about 25 miles southwest of the southern tip of the Sea of Galilee.

Revelation - Chapter 17

Revelation 17:1-18 KJV:

And there came one of the seven angels which had the seven vials, and talked with me, saying unto me, Come hither; I will shew unto thee the judgment of the great whore that sitteth upon many waters: 2 With whom the kings of the earth have committed fornication, and the inhabitants of the earth have been made drunk with the wine of her fornication. 3 So he carried me away in the spirit into the wilderness: and I saw a woman sit upon a scarlet coloured beast, full of names of blasphemy, having seven heads and ten horns. 4 And the woman was arrayed in purple and scarlet colour, and decked with gold and precious stones and pearls, having a golden cup in her hand full of abominations and filthiness of her fornication: 5 And upon her forehead was a name written, Mystery, Babylon The Great, The Mother Of Harlots And Abominations Of The earth. 6 And I saw the woman drunken with the blood of the saints, and with the blood of the martyrs of Jesus: and when I saw her, I wondered with great admiration. 7 And the angel said unto me, Wherefore didst thou marvel?

I will tell thee the mystery of the woman, and of the beast that carrieth her, which hath the seven heads and ten horns. **8** *The beast that thou sawest was, and is not; and shall ascend out of the bottomless pit, and go into perdition: and they that dwell on the earth shall wonder, whose names were not written in the book of life from the foundation of the world, when they behold the beast that was, and is not, and yet is.* **9** *And here is the mind which hath wisdom. The seven heads are seven mountains, on which the woman sitteth.* **10** *And there are seven kings: five are fallen, and one is, and the other is not yet come; and when he cometh, he must continue a short space.* **11** *And the beast that was, and is not, even he is the eighth, and is of the seven, and goeth into perdition.* **12** *And the ten horns which thou sawest are ten kings, which have received no kingdom as yet; but receive power as kings one hour with the beast.* **13** *These have one mind, and shall give their power and strength unto the beast.* **14** *These shall make war with the Lamb, and the Lamb shall overcome them: for he is Lord of lords, and King of kings: and they that are with him are called, and chosen, and faithful.* **15** *And he saith unto me, The waters which thou sawest, where the whore sitteth, are peoples, and multitudes, and nations, and tongues.* **16** *And the ten horns which thou sawest upon the beast, these shall hate the whore, and shall make her desolate and naked, and shall eat her flesh, and burn her with fire.* **17** *For God hath put in their hearts to fulfil his will, and to agree, and give their kingdom unto the beast, until the words of God shall be fulfilled.* **18** *And the woman which thou sawest is that great city, which reigneth over the kings of the earth.*

The Middle East is the backdrop of most of the events John sees in the last days. The seven churches that Jesus addresses are in Turkey, the city of Jerusalem is where the witnesses prophesy, the 144,000 Jews are with Jesus on Mount Zion. It's where the final battle of Armageddon is held near the mountain in Israel called Megiddo. The fallen angels who were bound are released from the great river Euphrates, which flows through Syria and Iraq. So as I continue to understand Revelation as it relates to the last days, I have to constantly steer myself away from my American mindset and focus on the Middle East and what Jesus would have been showing and telling John.

What John is shown next gives further evidence for my hypothesis that most of the second half of Revelation is a retelling of specific events that actually took place in the first half. One of the angels who poured out the plagues comes over to talk to John and he basically says if you come with me, *"I will show you what is going to happen to the Notorious Prostitute, who sits upon the many waters of the world."* John is whisked away into the wilderness and shown a most horrifying creature. A woman who is dressed in red and purple, she's got on lots of expensive flashy jewelry, she's foul mouthed (she's drinking a goblet of obscenities), she's got blood coming out of the corners of her mouth, and she's drunk (John could see that she was drunk with the blood of the martyrs of Jesus). John just stands there in horror at this gaudy, awful creature. This "notorious prostitute" is referred to as Babylon the Great, mother of prostitutes and idol worship everywhere around the world.

Who is Babylon and why is her judgment so severe that almost three chapters are devoted to her destruction? While I have no intention of delving into a comprehensive history of ancient Babylon, I do want to concentrate on what makes her such an enemy of God. Most scholars don't believe the reference to Babylon in Revelation is the literal city that exists today; and I am inclined to agree. Modern day Babylon is a city mostly in ruins about 50 miles south of Baghdad - only a shell of its former days under multiple rulers. Given enough time, it could very well be as powerful and menacing as it used to be - we've seen that happen before with various other nations. But I personally think that it is not the actual city but the characteristics of that city which the angel is referring. Just an ordinary example of this would be the brand name of Kleenex. The Kleenex brand so captured the market with its product that people interchange its name with its product (or characteristic). People will ask, "Will you pass me a Kleenex?" What they really mean is "Will you pass me a tissue?" Babylon so captured the market on evil in God's eyes that if you were called Babylon, you were being called by its characteristic...evil. So, I want to look at the characteristics of ancient Babylon.

The original name of Babylon is Babel. If you are not familiar with that name, it is referred to in Genesis 11. Right in the middle of the list of the genealogy of Noah after the flood, there is the story of Noah's great, great grandson, Nimrod, who was the king of ancient Babylon or Babel. The story goes like this. The people had "one language and one speech" according to the scripture. In today's language that means the people on the earth at the time were all saying the same thing. There were no dissenting opinions. There were no political parties, no minority opposition, just one acceptable social behavior. Just one social norm. The only problem with all this unity and harmony that resulted in everyone getting along was an insidious act against God. With one goal they decided that they would build a city with a tower that would reach heaven. They were going to use bricks and dirt, materials God had given them, so that they could "make a name for themselves." They didn't want to be known by God's name, they wanted their own name. This was a haughty, arrogant act of rebellion. One that God was very familiar with. Satan destroyed his life and the life of millions of fallen angels that he convinced to follow him with the same ungrateful plan. He said, "I will exalt my throne above God's" - make a name for myself apart from God. There is no greater act of sin than rebellion. Ironically, we don't know any of the names of the people who were a part of this rebellion - they are nameless and faceless in scripture. The very thing they were trying to accomplish without God, making a name for themselves, caused them to lose their identity for all eternity.

God came down to see this city and tower that the people built. God said, *"Indeed the people are one and they all have one language, and this is what they begin to do; now nothing that they propose to do will be withheld from them."* It was then that God "confused their language," the consensus being that this is how and why foreign languages began. I imagine it happened as quickly as lightning flashes, everyone started wandering around trying to find another person they could understand and that could understand them. Perhaps, he rewired their thinking or their ability to empathize with each other. Perhaps, it was not just their linguistic differences that were altered but also their intellectual differences as well. In either case, God scattered this people across the earth so that he would not have to once again destroy them.

Fast forward to the end of the age, approximately 6,000 years - again, six being the number of man. After all God did to preserve the life of those original Babylonians this is what they have become in 6,000 years. A filthy prostitute, who performs all types of perversion to gain money and a name for herself, bent on murdering every dissenting voice of the people of God. I personally know women who've been prostitutes. This whore of Babylon is so awful, she gives prostitutes a bad name.

The angel is surprised that John is surprised with the sight of the prostitute but he goes on to describe who she is and the beast she is riding. John is not always told the meaning of the images he sees, probably because some of them literally are what they are, but in this chapter he is given details, John is told that the mystery of Babylon is that she is, in fact, a city. A great city which reigns over all the kings of the world.

The great prostitute is riding on a scarlet animal. A familiar one. It has seven heads and ten horns. This is the same description for the beast in Revelation 13, and Daniel 7 right down to the blasphemies written on its heads. The angel told Daniel this creature would be the last world power on the earth before Jesus returns. The seven heads are seven kings. The ten horns are ten kings the angel said had not come to power yet, at least not as of John's writing. Because of an immediate circumstance perhaps the second coming event, these ten kings or ten nations are given power for a brief time, long enough to sign a treaty with the beast. Of course, treachery and murder is really the goal as they are being deceived by satan. They betray the great prostitute. She thinks that they are still working with her but their hatred for her is deep. She is destroyed in one day and the merchants of the world mourn her loss.

Then the ten kings wage war against Jesus. This is the war of Armageddon - part of the judgment of God when the sixth plague is released in chapter 16. The kings of the earth go to war with Jesus. They lose.

Revelation - Chapter 18

And after these things I saw another angel come down from heaven, having great power; and the earth was lightened with his glory. 2 And he cried mightily with a strong voice, saying, Babylon the great is fallen, is fallen, and is become the habitation of devils, and the hold of every foul spirit, and a cage of every unclean and hateful bird. 3 For all nations have drunk of the wine of the wrath of her fornication, and the kings of the earth have committed fornication with her, and the merchants of the earth are waxed rich through the abundance of her delicacies. 4 And I heard another voice from heaven, saying, Come out of her, my people, that ye be not partakers of her sins, and that ye receive not of her plagues. 5 For her sins have reached unto heaven, and God hath remembered her iniquities. 6 Reward her even as she rewarded you, and double unto her double according to her works: in the cup which she hath filled fill to her double. 7 How much she hath glorified herself, and lived deliciously, so much torment and sorrow give her: for she saith in her heart, I sit a queen, and am no widow, and shall see no sorrow. **8** *Therefore shall her plagues come in one day, death, and mourning, and famine; and she shall be utterly burned with fire: for strong is the Lord God who judgeth her.* **9** *And the kings of the earth, who have committed fornication and lived deliciously with her, shall bewail her, and lament for her, when they shall see the smoke of her burning,* **10** *Standing afar off for the fear of her torment, saying, Alas, alas that great city Babylon, that mighty city! for in one hour is thy judgment come.* **11** *And the merchants of the earth shall weep and mourn over her; for no man buyeth their merchandise any more:* **12** *The merchandise of gold, and silver, and precious stones, and of pearls, and fine linen, and purple, and silk, and scarlet, and all thyine wood, and all manner vessels of ivory, and all manner vessels of most precious wood, and of brass, and iron, and marble,* **13** *And cinnamon, and odours, and ointments, and frankincense, and wine, and oil, and fine flour, and wheat, and beasts, and sheep, and horses, and chariots, and slaves, and souls of men.* **14** *And the fruits that thy soul lusted after are departed from thee, and all things which were dainty and are departed from thee, and thou shalt find them no more at all.* **15** *The merchants of these things, which were made rich by her, shall stand afar off for the fear of her torment, weeping and wailing,* **16** *And saying, Alas, alas that great city, that was clothed in fine linen, and purple, and scarlet, and decked with gold, and precious stones, and pearls!* **17** *For in one hour so great riches is come to nought. And every shipmaster, and all the company in ships, and sailors, and as many as trade by sea, stood afar off,* **18** *And cried* *when they saw the smoke of her burning, saying, What city is like unto this great city! 19 And they cast dust on their heads, and cried, weeping and wailing, saying, Alas, alas that great city, wherein were made rich all that had ships in the sea by reason of her costliness! for in one hour is she made desolate. 20 Rejoice over her, thou heaven, and ye holy apostles and prophets; for God hath avenged you on her. 21 And a mighty angel took up a stone like a great millstone, and cast it into the sea, saying, Thus with violence shall that great city Babylon be thrown down, and shall be found no more at all. 22 And the voice of harpers, and musicians, and of pipers, and trumpeters, shall be heard no more at all in thee; and no craftsman, of whatsoever craft he be, shall be found any more in thee; and the sound of a millstone shall be heard no more at all in thee; 23 And the light of a candle shall shine no more at all in thee; and the voice of the bridegroom and of the bride shall be heard no more at all in thee: for thy merchants were the great men of the earth; for by thy sorceries were all nations deceived. 24 And in her was found the blood of prophets, and of saints, and of all that were slain upon the earth.*

John sees another angel with great authority coming down from heaven. His sole purpose seems to be to express to John the magnitude of Babylon's sins and the magnitude of her destruction. The angel again warns about being associated with this horrible city. If Babylon is so bad why would anyone have to be warned to stay away from her? Because like most things that are detestable to God in this world, satan has dressed them up to look really cool and amazing. He is the great deceiver and if you forget this or have no concept of this, you will find yourself fighting against God every time.

The angel warns that this city will be consumed with death, mourning, and famine. In one hour it will be destroyed by a great fire. For the record, in John's day, and even a hundred years ago, it wasn't really possible to destroy a city in an hour. But the weapons of today could do just that and more. All the merchants of the earth who have done business with her will weep and mourn at her torment. No more gold, silver, precious stones, or pearls. No more fine linen, and silk from the city known for being the center of cultural activity. No more ivory, costly wood, bronze, iron and marble. No more spices, or wine, olive oil, flour or wheat. Even the captains and sailors who make their living from the sea will exclaim, was there ever a city like this great city? After being the center of the world and the host city for all the influential people, there would be no more galas, no more shopping here. No more cattle and sheep, and horses. And no more human trafficking! How odd that the angel would add this as if it were as common as all the other trading done in the city. Perhaps, that was the point, anything could be bought and sold in a city like Babylon. This was no ordinary city. It was a city full of pride and corruption. This city was an abomination to the Lord, yet it enjoyed the adoration of merchants from every nation around the world.

I thought I would give it a try - see if I could figure out what city best describes the great city of Babylon in the 21st century. There have been several cities in the history of humankind which could have claimed this title.

One of the most noted was the city actually called Babylon under Nebuchadnezzar who conquered Jerusalem. God had warned his people, Israel, that if they continued to rebel against him, he would not let them stay in the land he had given them. God allowed this pagan king to destroy the city of Jerusalem and take captive the best of everything that was left. Daniel was one of the young men from Israel who was taken and groomed for the king's palace. The book of Daniel gives us an inside look at this pagan king's reign. But the great Babylon that the angel refers to is not one from the past. The great Babylon from Revelation is one that has emerged in the last days.

Since the focus of Revelation is on the Middle East, I thought maybe I should turn my attention there to find Babylon. The city of Aleppo in Syria was an unfortunate possibility. You wouldn't recognize it today but the city of Aleppo was once called the merchant city of the Middle East. It was a cultural hub known for its diversity. Arabs, Muslims, Christians, Armenians, Jews peacefully co-existed. Today, it is a war-torn shell. Between the rebels fighting a civil war and the bombing by the Russians and the U.S., Aleppo has been completely destroyed. This civil war in Syria started in 2012. No one expected that it would last over eight years. While it is very sad to see the before and after pictures of what was once a thriving metropolis, Aleppo was not destroyed in a day and it is not, nor has it ever been considered, a city that has reigned over all the nations of the world.

So I thought I would google the most influential city in the world. A couple of years ago, according to Forbes Magazine, London was ranked first and New York City was a close second. In 2018, New York City edged out London. London's influence and history of being the "model" for the world's legal and judiciary systems could not compete any longer with New York's impressive list: the global leader in media, advertisement

116

and the music industry, home to most of the world's top investment banks and hedge funds, most of the wealthiest people in the world live here - approximately 680 billionaires call New York home, the hub of the fashion industry, and home of Wall Street and the United Nations.

Now that I had the number one city, although this is not a contest I would want to win, I looked again at what God had to say about it. Babylon was a dwelling for demons and every impure spirit on the earth. The merchants of the world grew rich from her excess. The nations were drunk with the maddening wine of all her adultery...wait...what? How can a city commit adultery? I believe this is key to the identity of the city of Babylon. The only other time God accused a city of committing adultery was when He spoke of his people Israel. Read the book of Isaiah. God said that Israel was so infatuated with her enemies that she was like a prostitute who didn't even charge for her service. In fact, she paid other nations to have economic and cultural relationships with her. Israel had left her first love, which was God. If Babylon is a city that is also well known to others as belonging to God, New York City would be a good guess.

I'm sure every secular New Yorker would vehemently reject the notion that God had anything to do with their success. They would protest, "Don't you know who we are? Don't you remember our theme song?" "I Did it My Way." We have made a name for ourselves! Sound familiar? This is what the ancient city of Babel said.

America was founded by fallible, flawed, human beings who said of themselves we are, "One nation, under God." Even when America was flatly denying it, the nations of the world were hating us because we were a Christian nation. The fact that people in this country don't remember or want to remember that this is our heritage does not negate this fact. The notorious prostitute is not an abomination because she is worse than other cities or nations, she's an abomination because she has committed the sin of spiritual adultery.

This great city that rejected her first love just like Israel did thousands of years ago, will be thrown down, never to be found again. Who will destroy her? Just like Israel, it won't be God but all of her previous lovers who secretly hated her because of her success. She was greatly loved by God but now, at this time in history, she has broken completely away from her covering, her protection. She is vulnerable and they know it.

I realize that calling New York City "Babylon" is an offensive thing to say considering all the great ministries and goodwill that has come out of this place. Perhaps you should consider a different New York City. One where there are no more goodhearted people, no ministries, no Christians. Anything good and righteous has been removed - gone with Jesus when he returned. Now what do you have left? Babylon. The punishment of Babylon is not for the righteous - that is the only thing that has kept any ungodly city from being destroyed already. The punishment of Babylon is for the wicked. Specifically, those who rebelled and continue to rebel against God and his Word no matter what plagues and destruction come on the earth.

If you are still struggling to believe that your favorite city to visit for all things entertainment is the new Babylon, then consider what they recently added to their collection of rebellion. A 50-foot arch of the temple of Baal honoring the symbol of pagan deity. And, how, exactly, did one worship Baal in ancient times? By committing sexual immorality and killing their children on the altar of human sacrifice. Who was the leader in destroying babies up to the moment of birth? New York City. Babylon.

Obviously, this is a theory and I would like to be wrong. However, the Bible gives us a good indication of what happens when a people who enjoyed the blessings of God, turns its back and begins to take credit for its own success.

Revelation - Chapter 19

Revelation 19:1-21 KJV:

And after these things I heard a great voice of much people in heaven, saying, Alleluia; Salvation, and glory, and honour, and power, unto the Lord our God: **2** For true and righteous are his judgments: for he hath judged the great whore, which did corrupt the earth with her fornication, and hath avenged the blood of his servants at her hand. **3** And again they said, Alleluia And her smoke rose up for ever and ever. **4** And the four and twenty elders and the four beasts fell down and worshipped God that sat on the throne, saying, Amen; Alleluia. **5** And a voice came out of the throne, saying, Praise our God, all ye his servants, and ye that fear him, both small and great. **6** And I heard as it were the voice of a great multitude, and as the voice of many waters, and as the voice of mighty thunderings, saying, Alleluia: for the Lord God omnipotent reigneth. **7** Let us be glad and rejoice, and give honour to him: for the marriage of the Lamb is come, and his wife hath made herself ready. **8** And to her was granted that she should be arrayed in fine linen, clean and white: for the fine linen *is the righteousness of saints. 9 And he saith unto me, Write, Blessed are they which are called unto the marriage supper of the Lamb. And he saith unto me, These are the true sayings of God. 10 And I fell at his feet to worship him. And he said unto me, See thou do it not: I am thy fellowservant, and of thy brethren that have the testimony of Jesus: worship God: for the testimony of Jesus is the spirit of prophecy. 11 And I saw heaven opened, and behold a white horse; and he that sat upon him was called Faithful and True, and in righteousness he doth judge and make war. 12 His eyes were as a flame of fire, and on his head were many crowns; and he had a name written, that no man knew, but he himself. 13 And he was clothed with a vesture dipped in blood: and his name is called The Word of God. 14 And the armies which were in heaven followed him upon white horses, clothed in fine linen, white and clean. 15 And out of his mouth goeth a sharp sword, that with it he should smite the nations: and he shall rule them with a rod of iron: and he treadeth the winepress of the fierceness and wrath of Almighty God. 16 And he hath on his vesture and on his thigh a name written, King Of Kings, And Lord Of Lords. 17 And I saw an angel standing in the sun; and he cried with a loud voice, saying to all the fowls that fly in the midst of heaven, Come and gather yourselves together unto the supper of the great God; 18 That ye may eat the flesh of kings, and the flesh of captains, and the flesh of mighty men, and the flesh of horses, and of them that sit on them, and the flesh of all men, both free and bond, both small and great. 19 And I saw the beast, and the kings of the earth, and their armies, gathered*

together to make war against him that sat on the horse,
*and against his army. **20** And the beast was taken, and*
with him the false prophet that wrought miracles before
him, with which he deceived them that had received the
mark of the beast, and them that worshipped his image.
These both were cast alive into a lake of fire burning with
*brimstone. **21** And the remnant were slain with the sword*
of him that sat upon the horse, which sword proceeded out
of his mouth: and all the fowls were filled with their flesh.

Chapter 19 begins with what looks like a contrast between the
world's reaction to the fall of Babylon and heaven's reaction.
There were expressions of great loss from the merchants of the
earth as they mourned over her destruction in chapter 18. But
in heaven, there is great praise to the Lord God for bringing
judgment, and avenging the blood of His prophets and martyrs.
What has been done in the shadows has finally come to the light.
This city, directly and indirectly, has been responsible for their
murders and for corrupting the whole world!

Who is rejoicing that this city has finally been judged? John
says it's the four living beings, the elders around the throne and
the great multitude. You remember them - the number too vast
to count? That same great multitude no doubt that arrived in
heaven after Jesus and his angels appeared in the sky in chapter
six. The fall of Babylon happens after the people of God are in
heaven.

They are worshiping and praising God with all their might.
They are glad for this great victory and they are also very excited.
You see, they are about to get ready for an event and they have
been waiting for a lifetime. An event unlike any ever seen in

heaven or on earth. They are preparing for the marriage supper of the Lamb. They say, *"Alleluia! For the Lord God Omnipotent reigns! Let us be glad and rejoice and give him glory, for the marriage of the Lamb has come, and his wife has made herself ready."*

Now here is where it gets a little tricky. If the multitudes are the ones shouting this praise and adoration about God and about being invited to the marriage supper, who exactly is the bride if not these? Why didn't they say "we" have made ourselves ready? The next verse reveals who the bride of Christ truly is; the wife of the Lamb are those who are dressed in fine linen, which represents their righteous acts on earth.

There's an old song by Mahalia Jackson, a gospel singer from the 30's, called "Rusty Old Halo. Here are the words:

I know a man, rich as a king, still he just won't give his neighbor a thing
His day will come, I'll make a bet. He'll get to heaven and here's what he'll get

A rusty old halo, a skinny white cloud, second-hand wings full of patches
Rusty old halo, skinny white cloud, robe that's so wooly it scratches

This is a humorously, sobering explanation that is apparently quite accurate. There will be those in heaven who just barely made it (rusty old halo). Paul, the apostle, warns about how we should build our lives in 1 Corinthians 3, *"There is going to come a time of testing at Christ's Judgment Day to see what kind of material each builder has used. Everyone's work will be put through the fire so that all can see whether or not it keeps its value, and what was really accomplished. Then every workman who has built on the foundation with the right materials, and whose work still stands, will get his pay. But if the house he has built burns up, he will have a great loss. He himself will be saved, but like a man escaping through a wall of flames."*

And, there will be those who dedicated their whole lives to God. They gave, they served, and they sacrificed. Psalms 37 says, *"Day by day the Lord observes the good deeds done by the godly, and gives them eternal rewards."* Everyone in heaven will be children of God but Revelation suggests that the ones clothed in righteous acts will be the bride of Christ.

Then the angel who has been guiding John through these last events tells John to write down *"Blessed are those invited to the marriage supper of the Lamb!"* The angel looks at John and says, "These are the true sayings of God." In other words, "This is what God is saying to you." At this, John seems to be overwhelmed. He has seen a lot of horrible things but it is this announcement that makes him overcome with emotion. He falls down in worship at this angel's feet. Of course, the angel is like whoa, don't do that! He was probably shocked that John didn't recognize him! Surprisingly, this angel reveals to John that he is not an angel at all. He basically says, "I'm a Christian just like you!" Perhaps the brilliance of his righteous acts (fine linens) threw John off. Perhaps it was the fact that this angel (really a believer) was one of the seven who emerged from the temple of God to receive a bowl to pour out on the earth. Can you imagine John's surprise? You mean ordinary human beings are able to get that close to the one sitting on the throne?!

So what is the groom doing while the bride is getting ready? John says, *"Now I saw heaven opened, and behold, a white horse. And He who sat on him was called Faithful and True, and in righteousness He judges and makes war. His eyes were like a flame of fire, and on His head were many crowns. He had a name written that no one knew except himself. He was clothed with a robe dipped in blood, and His name is called The Word of God."* The words of a song I once heard at a prayer meeting came to mind as I read this. It went, "Woe to the enemy of the king on his wedding day!" Jesus has rescued his bride and now he and his army of warriors are about to go to battle against those who tried to harm her. This is the Battle at Armageddon - the war that is mentioned in Chapter 16.

I remember pastors preaching that the bride of Christ is the army going into battle with him. I imagine this conclusion was reached because the army is dressed in fine linen just like John describes the bride a few verses earlier. However, the great prostitute Babylon was also dressed in fine linen and we know how silly that would be to suggest that the great harlot is also part of the Lord's army. Jesus has more than enough warriors to fight with him - look at the stars in the universe - he doesn't need to enlist his bride to help him kill his enemies.

However, I do remember reading in young Colton Burpo's book, Heaven Is For Real, about him seeing the end of the age (again - the spirit world is outside of time) and he said he saw believers on horses with Jesus going to battle. Actually, I can so imagine almost every Christian male friend (and a few female friends) that I know who would be so stoked to be a part of that battle. I can just hear them asking Jesus if they can "please, please" go with him when he defeats his enemies. So, it's not hard to believe that Colton and other believers saw Christians on horses going into battle. Come to think of it, being a part of a battle against all that is evil, that you absolutely can't lose is quite appealing. But the bride is not fighting, she is getting herself ready for the marriage supper of the Lamb.

The beast, the kings of the world, and their armies gather there to fight after the sixth bowl is poured out. But it is the seventh bowl that seals their doom. The seventh plague or bowl is poured out in Chapter 16 and a voice from the Temple in heaven says, "It is finished!" Perhaps, this is what Jesus meant when he said it the first time as he hung from the cross. We thought he meant his work on the cross was complete but perhaps Jesus was already there in the spirit at the end of the age with a sword in his mouth pronouncing the final judgment on the enemies of God. The beast, the false prophet (which was the second beast in Chapter 16) and the armies of the world are defeated. The beast and false prophet are captured and cast into the lake of fire. The misguided rebellious human armies of the world are killed and the birds of the air feast on their flesh.

Revelation - Chapter 20

Revelation 20:1-15 KJV:

*And I saw an angel come down from heaven, having the key of the bottomless pit and a great chain in his hand. **2** And he laid hold on the dragon, that old serpent, which is the Devil, and Satan, and bound him a thousand years, **3** And cast him into the bottomless pit, and shut him up, and set a seal upon him, that he should deceive the nations no more, till the thousand years should be fulfilled: and after that he must be loosed a little season. **4** And I saw thrones, and they sat upon them, and judgment was given unto them: and I saw the souls of them that were beheaded for the witness of Jesus, and for the word of God, and which had not worshipped the beast, neither his image, neither had received his mark upon their foreheads, or in their hands; and they lived and reigned with Christ a thousand years. **5** But the rest of the dead lived not again until the thousand years were finished. This is the first resurrection. **6** Blessed and holy is he that hath part in the first resurrection: on such the second death hath no power, but they shall be priests of God and of Christ, and* *shall reign with him a thousand years.* **7** *And when the thousand years are expired, Satan shall be loosed out of his prison,* **8** *And shall go out to deceive the nations which are in the four quarters of the earth, Gog, and Magog, to gather them together to battle: the number of whom is as the sand of the sea.* **9** *And they went up on the breadth of the earth, and compassed the camp of the saints about, and the beloved city: and fire came down from God out of heaven, and devoured them.* **10** *And the devil that deceived them was cast into the lake of fire and brimstone, where the beast and the false prophet are, and shall be tormented day and night for ever and ever.* **11** *And I saw a great white throne, and him that sat on it, from whose face the earth and the heaven fled away; and there was found no place for them.* **12** *And I saw the dead, small and great, stand before God; and the books were opened: and another book was opened, which is the book of life: and the dead were judged out of those things which were written in the books, according to their works.* **13** *And the sea gave up the dead which were in it; and death and hell delivered up the dead which were in them: and they were judged every man according to their works.* **14** *And death and hell were cast into the lake of fire. This is the second death.* **15** *And whosoever was not found written in the book of life was cast into the lake of fire.*

The battle of Armageddon has ended and the beast and the false prophet have been cast into the lake of fire. Don't you find it strange that the dragon, satan, was not at the battle? Why is he conspicuously absent from the fighting? Because he's a deceiver, not a fighter. But his day has come as well.

John sees an angel - not a super angel, just an angel - who grabs hold of satan, binds him up and throws him into the bottomless pit. He is held there for a thousand years so that he won't be able to deceive the nations anymore.

Why only a thousand years? Why not forever? Well, it seems that God wants to specifically reward those whose lives were cut short when they were martyred for Christ. Before he ends this age and we move into the next chapter of life on earth, he gives back the lives of those who lost the experience to live and love on earth. This reminds me of the scripture that says, "Those who trust in him will never be disappointed." Anyone who loses his life for God's sake will be given back much more - and eternal life.

Jesus also appoints judges from among the redeemed during these 1,000 years. This is very telling of the nature of God. Of all the occupations in the world, the one that John sees after the slate has been wiped clean of corruption is that of judges. God loves justice and mercy. No more political favors to get a seat on the bench. No, this job is for those who have the wisdom and understanding given to them by God. And God makes sure they are the ones over this important office.

What John is seeing now in Chapter 20 is the continuation of life on earth. God never intended for there to be an end. He expected that the human race (perhaps with Adam being the head) would rule and reign over earth just like God ruled and reigned over the universe. As you will see, his plan has not changed, only this time, the new earth will be ruled by the second Adam - the one who obeyed. Jesus Christ.

It is so sad today to see people living outrageously in their quest to experience life to the fullest. They make compromises and choices in these few short years that affect them for all eternity. They reach their goals by lying and cheating and destroying anyone in their way because they erroneously believe that this is all there is (satan's greatest weapon of deception). While those who believed God and loved him more than their own temporary lives are reigning with Jesus for a thousand years, those who sold their souls to the devil, or just rejected eternal life with Jesus, are being tormented in the fires of hell, in the same prison cells as the evil beings who are there waiting to be judged for the choices they made.

After the thousand years, satan is released to do what he does best - deceive anyone who is still willing to discard the truth for a lie. Everyone who lives on earth gets the same opportunity to receive rewards for their faith. They also get the same opportunity to choose life with God. Those who choose death after this thousand year reign, will once again be weeded out so that the beginning of a new age will be filled with people who truly love God. It's another uneven fight between God and all the armies of the world, worked into a frenzy by satan - Gog and Magog. By the way, that is what I believe the phrase Gog and Magog mean. An uneven fight between God and all the armies of the world. It would be like someone saying, "It's World War II again!" They are simply stating that whatever is happening has the same characteristics of World War II. So what is Gog and Magog? It's a well-known battle in ancient history that ended abruptly for those opposing Israel. So, the characteristics of Gog and Magog happened at the war of Armageddon and again in this chapter. The enemies of God surround Jerusalem but this time it's just a flash of fire from heaven that devours them. Done.

The devil is finally cast into the lake of fire and now the White

Throne Judgment begins. This is where everyone who was not a part of the first resurrection is brought alive to be judged for what they had done on earth. The seas give up their dead, the earth gives up her dead and the underworld (hell) gives us their (spiritual) dead. Spirit and body joined together again for the final judgment. This is considered the second resurrection. Don't let anyone tell you that you cease to exist when you die. This is by far the most damaging idea you could ever have. If I am wrong and I have lived a Godly life only to cease to exist, I haven't really lost anything. Loving people and loving God has been extremely rewarding. But if you are wrong, the consequences are disastrous. It's eternal death away from God and all that is good, thrown into a tormenting lake of fire.

John says, *"I saw the dead, great and small, standing before God; and The Books were opened, including the Book of Life. And the dead were judged according to the things written in The Books, each according to the deeds he had done."* Please understand, the books opened are not to decide if your good deeds outweighed your bad in order for you to go to heaven. No, the books determine what level of punishment is awaiting you based on your deeds. The only ones who may enter heaven are those whose names are written in the Book of Life. Whose book is it? The Lamb's Book of Life. Who is the Lamb? Jesus Christ is the Lamb that was slain. After seeing this, John says, *"Blessed and Holy are those who share in the first resurrection!"*

Let me reiterate, the first resurrection is the resurrection of every believer in Jesus Christ who has been given eternal life either by being caught up to meet Jesus when he returns or having died on the earth. God brought Jesus back from the dead. He was the "firstfruits" as I mentioned in earlier chapters, so that we would have a frame of reference - we would be assured that we too would rise again from the dead.

If you truly believe that Jesus died for your sins you will not have to worry about whether you have done enough good deeds to outweigh your bad. We will not be judged like the rest of humankind who are gambling with their very lives by thinking they can escape hell or get to heaven by doing good deeds. No, we get to heaven because of our faith in Jesus. He paid the penalty for our sin.

Revelation - Chapter 21

Revelation 21:1-27 KJV:

And I saw a new heaven and a new earth: for the first heaven and the first earth were passed away; and there was no more sea. 2 And I John saw the holy city, new Jerusalem, coming down from God out of heaven, prepared as a bride adorned for her husband. 3 And I heard a great voice out of heaven saying, Behold, the tabernacle of God is with men, and he will dwell with them, and they shall be his people, and God himself shall be with them, and be their God. 4 And God shall wipe away all tears from their eyes; and there shall be no more death, neither sorrow, nor crying, neither shall there be any more pain: for the former things are passed away. 5 And he that sat upon the throne said, Behold, I make all things new. And he said unto me, Write: for these words are true and faithful. 6 And he said unto me, It is done. I am Alpha and Omega, the beginning and the end. I will give unto him that is athirst of the fountain of the water of life freely. 7 He that overcometh shall inherit all things; and I will be his God, and he shall be my son. 8 But the fearful, and unbelieving, and the abominable, and murderers, and whoremongers, and sorcerers, and idolaters, and all liars, shall have their part in the lake which burneth with fire and brimstone: which is the second death. *9 And there came unto me one of the seven angels which had the seven vials full of the seven last plagues, and talked with me, saying, Come hither, I will shew thee the bride, the Lamb's wife. 10 And he carried me away in the spirit to a great and high mountain, and shewed me that great city, the holy Jerusalem, descending out of heaven from God, 11 Having the glory of God: and her light was like unto a stone most precious, even like a jasper stone, clear as crystal; 12 And had a wall great and high, and had twelve gates, and at the gates twelve angels, and names written thereon, which are the names of the twelve tribes of the children of Israel: 13 On the east three gates; on the north three gates; on the south three gates; and on the west three gates. 14 And the wall of the city had twelve foundations, and in them the names of the twelve apostles of the Lamb. 15 And he that talked with me had a golden reed to measure the city, and the gates thereof, and the wall thereof. 16 And the city lieth foursquare, and the length is as large as the breadth: and he measured the city with the reed, twelve thousand furlongs. The length and the breadth and the height of it are equal. 17 And he measured the wall thereof, an hundred and forty and four cubits, according to the measure of a man, that is, of the angel. 18 And the building of the wall of it was of jasper: and the city was pure gold, like unto clear glass. 19 And the foundations of the wall of the city were garnished with all manner of precious stones. The first foundation*

*was jasper; the second, sapphire; the third, a chalcedony;
the fourth, an emerald; 20 The fifth, sardonyx; the sixth,
sardius; the seventh, chrysolyte; the eighth, beryl; the ninth,
a topaz; the tenth, a chrysoprasus; the eleventh, a jacinth;
the twelfth, an amethyst. 21 And the twelve gates were
twelve pearls: every several gate was of one pearl: and
the street of the city was pure gold, as it were transparent
glass. 22 And I saw no temple therein: for the Lord God
Almighty and the Lamb are the temple of it. 23 And the
city had no need of the sun, neither of the moon, to shine in
it: for the glory of God did lighten it, and the Lamb is the
light thereof. 24 And the nations of them which are saved
shall walk in the light of it: and the kings of the earth do
bring their glory and honour into it. 25 And the gates of it
shall not be shut at all by day: for there shall be no night
there. 26 And they shall bring the glory and honour of
the nations into it. 27 And there shall in no wise enter
into it any thing that defileth, neither whatsoever worketh
abomination, or maketh a lie: but they which are written
in the Lamb's book of life.*

John sees a most magnificent sight! A new heaven and a new earth. And John is made aware that the sea does not exist any longer. There will be no more humongous bodies of water. Well, that sounds just fine to me. While I have been mesmerized by the sight, I have always been unnerved by the vastness of the water and what could potentially be under it. But I'm not sure how my beach-going, water-loving friends are going to feel about there being no more oceans. Perhaps, transparency is the reason there will no longer be oceans on earth. Nothing will be hidden any longer - not even under the water.

John then sees the Holy city coming out of heaven and a voice from the throne saying: *"Behold, the dwelling of God is with humanity, and he will take up residence with them, and they will be his people and God himself will be with them. And he will wipe away every tear from their eyes, and death will not exist any longer, and mourning or wailing or pain will not exist any longer. The former things have passed away."*

We have never known life like this before. We have been born into sin and our psyche has been shaped in the iniquity all around us. A world with no death, no pain, no more sorrow. Why would we ever hold on so tightly to this life we currently have? Perhaps because of fear of the unknown. We can't even imagine it, which is why God tells John that he can truly believe him when he says, "See, I make all things new." This is the message woven through every event of Revelation. You can trust him, just believe. Don't be a coward, just believe.

That is why faith in God is such a valuable commodity in heaven. It is equivalent to money on earth. The more faith you had on earth the richer you are in heaven. People who don't know God have always had contempt for those who do. They think religion is for the weak-minded. This of course is another deception that satan has used to destroy people. The truth is, it takes a person of great courage and fortitude to live in this fallen world with nothing but death and disappointment at every turn and still believe that God loves them and has all this planned for their eternal life. The truly weak-minded are the ones who go along with every lie they see or hear across the airwaves -perpetrated by satan. How amazing will it be to see this earth fully alive and void of any death or deception?

One of the angels who poured out one of the seven last plagues

136

says to John, "*Come, I will show you the bride, the wife of the Lamb.*" He carries John's spirit away to a high mountain and he showed him the holy city of Jerusalem coming down from heaven. The earthly Jerusalem has always held a special place in God's heart. It's probably where the Garden of Eden is located. Since this city coming down from heaven looks like Jerusalem to John, God must have patterned the earthly Jerusalem after the heavenly Jerusalem. This city has caused the most contentious fighting on earth. For these religions: Judaism, Christianity, Islam, this is the center of the world. No wonder satan has continued to stir up strife concerning this city - it probably reminds him of heaven and what he lost.

Since satan has been dealt with and all rebellion has been removed from earth, God can now do what he wanted to do all along - come and dwell among his creation. This is the home of the Father, the Son, the Holy Spirit and the wife of the Lamb. Jesus said, "*In my father's house are many mansions...I go to prepare a place for you and if I go and prepare a place, I will come again to receive you unto myself, that where I am you may be also.*"

This city is absolutely stunning. It is made of pure gold and has the appearance of glass. The precious stones and every magnificent gem you have ever seen on earth, and many you have never seen, are intricately placed in this structure. There are twelve gates to this city, each gate made from a single pearl; and there is a mighty angel at each gate to welcome you. There are some things that are conspicuously absent. There is no temple - there is no coming to God in fear and trembling. The city of God is the temple now and the Son with his bride live with him. There is no sun in the sky - this city, the New Jerusalem, lights the whole world all by itself. There is no night - Jesus will be the lamp that triggers the time to rest. The gates will never shut and the rulers of the earth (those who have been redeemed) will bring their Glory, and add their light, when they come in and go out. And no unclean, detestable practice or falsehood will ever enter into it - ever.

Revelation - Chapter 22

Revelation 22:1-21 KJV:

And he shewed me a pure river of water of life, clear as crystal, proceeding out of the throne of God and of the Lamb. 2 In the midst of the street of it, and on either side of the river, was there the tree of life, which bare twelve manner of fruits, and yielded her fruit every month: and the leaves of the tree were for the healing of the nations. 3 And there shall be no more curse: but the throne of God and of the Lamb shall be in it; and his servants shall serve him: 4 And they shall see his face; and his name shall be in their foreheads. 5 And there shall be no night there; and they need no candle, neither light of the sun; for the Lord God giveth them light: and they shall reign for ever and ever. 6 And he said unto me, These sayings are faithful and true: and the Lord God of the holy prophets sent his angel to shew unto his servants the things which must shortly be done. 7 Behold, I come quickly: blessed is he that keepeth the sayings of the prophecy of this book. 8 And I John saw these things, and heard them. And when I had heard and seen, I fell down to worship before the feet of the angel

*which shewed me these things. **9** Then saith he unto me,
See thou do it not: for I am thy fellowservant, and of thy
brethren the prophets, and of them which keep the sayings
of this book: worship God. **10** And he saith unto me, Seal
not the sayings of the prophecy of this book: for the time
is at hand. **11** He that is unjust, let him be unjust still:
and he which is filthy, let him be filthy still: and he that
is righteous, let him be righteous still: and he that is holy,
let him be holy still. **12** And, behold, I come quickly; and
my reward is with me, to give every man according as his
work shall be. **13** I am Alpha and Omega, the beginning
and the end, the first and the last. **14** Blessed are they that
do his commandments, that they may have right to the tree
of life, and may enter in through the gates into the city. **15**
For without are dogs, and sorcerers, and whoremongers,
and murderers, and idolaters, and whosoever loveth and
maketh a lie. **16** I Jesus have sent mine angel to testify
unto you these things in the churches. I am the root and
the offspring of David, and the bright and morning star.
17 And the Spirit and the bride say, Come. And let him
that heareth say, Come. And let him that is athirst come.
And whosoever will, let him take the water of life freely.
18 For I testify unto every man that heareth the words
of the prophecy of this book, If any man shall add unto
these things, God shall add unto him the plagues that are
written in this book: **19** And if any man shall take away
from the words of the book of this prophecy, God shall take
away his part out of the book of life, and out of the holy
city, and from the things which are written in this book.
20 He which testifieth these things saith, Surely I come*

quickly. Amen. Even so, come, Lord Jesus. 21 The grace of our Lord Jesus Christ be with you all. Amen.

This is the final chapter of Revelation and I am happy to report that we win! Who is the "we" to which I'm referring? It is the "whosoever" that believes in Jesus. ***"God so loved the world that he gave his only begotten son that whosoever believes in him shall not perish but have everlasting life.*** Jesus, God's living, breathing letter to humankind, came to earth to not only show us what God was like, but to show us how much God loved us. In dying for us Jesus assured us that we would live with him. And what a life. No pain, no sorrow, no sickness, only love and beauty. We get to rule the nations that come upon the earth after us, and we get to enjoy for all eternity the creativity of God's infinite imagination. Not only will death be a thing of the past but so will boredom and mundane living. And think about it, we are a unique people indeed for we came out of the great tribulation of a fallen earth. No one from this point forward will ever experience what we experienced. We will have quite the story to tell to future generations. This is what's awaiting us if we continue to remain faithful until the end of this age. Revelation is not just about the end of time, it is about the beginning of eternity.

The believer (whom John thought was an angel) shows John a pure river that is crystal clear. It proceeds from the throne of God and the Lamb right down through the center of the city. In the middle of the street on either side of the river is the tree of life. The tree of life bears 12 different kinds of fruit, one new fruit each month, and the leaves on this tree will be the medicine for the world. No more sorcery or witchcraft - the root word being "pharmakia" - where we get the word "pharmacy." No more humans taking matters in their own hands, trying to heal themselves. Jesus will provide healing for all the nations on earth, just like God planned from the beginning, before the fall. Probably every single day of his three years of ministry on earth, Jesus, the second Adam, healed those he encountered who were sick; and he saved those who came to him that were spiritually lost - even up to the very day he died. His love for humanity has not changed.

As John is taking this all in, *"Then the angel said to me, 'These words are trustworthy and true: I am coming soon!' God, who tells his prophets what the future holds, has sent his angel to tell you this will happen soon. Blessed are those who believe it and all else written in the scroll."*

Jesus relays to John the most important message of Revelation, that he is coming soon and that his words can be trusted! John doesn't know quite what to do when he receives this message so he just falls down in worship again at this angel's feet. Now, a second time a believer has to tell John, "No, no, don't worship me, I'm just a man like you." Actually, he tells John he's just a prophet like other human prophets that John knows on earth. Now that's fascinating. We will still have the same gifts we were given on earth when we get to heaven! This prophet who spoke for God on earth is still speaking for God in heaven. How cool is that! I think I already knew this but somehow it has more significance when I consider gifts and talents that are not commonly thought to be eternal. We expect that singers will be singing in heaven and musicians will be playing instruments in heaven but if you have a gift for hospitality, will we be having parties at your house in heaven? We probably will! The implications are staggering because in heaven the human

142

limitations are gone! Perhaps this is what this prophet of God means when he further tells John that when the time comes those who are holy will continue on in greater holiness!

The rest of this last book of Revelation is a continuation of Jesus's warnings. Unlike Daniel's instructions, John is told not to seal up this book because the time of its fulfillment is very close. And while those who are holy will continue on in greater holiness as I stated above, those who are doing wrong, will do it more and more.

Through this angel/prophet of God, Jesus continues to reinforce that he is coming soon and that he is bringing rewards to everyone according to the deeds he has done. This will be a good day for some and a bad day for others as we have learned so far. Here are his last words to John:

"Look, I am coming soon! My reward is with me, and I will give to each person according to what they have done. I am the Alpha and the Omega, the First and the Last, the Beginning and the End.

"Blessed are those who wash their robes, that they may have the right to the tree of life and may go through the gates into the city. Outside are the dogs, those who practice magic arts, the sexually immoral, the murderers, the idolaters and everyone who loves and practices falsehood.

Did you notice that Jesus just made a distinction between being inside the city and outside the city? This is a curious thing. He can't be talking about Christians inside and sinners outside because sin has already been dealt with at the White Throne Judgment, remember? Those who rebelled against God and his Son have been cast into the lake of fire along with satan and all the fallen angels. So who are these outside the city with these obvious sinful natures? Ok, I'm going for it. Perhaps, these are Christians who barely made it into heaven.

We talked about them earlier. Jesus talked about them too. Now don't be offended (offense is the new black). Yes, I know, Jesus calls them dogs, and murderers, and sexually immoral. But apparently, they know him and He knows them. And I can guarantee that anyone who finds themselves outside the beautiful city of God may be upset for a minute (the scripture says there will be weeping and gnashing of teeth...probably when they realize what they gave up just to satisfy their own lust) but they wouldn't trade it for the world. A dog outside God's city is better than a king in the lake of fire. Jesus continues...

"I, Jesus, have sent my angel to you to tell the churches all these things. I am both David's Root and his Descendant. I am the bright Morning Star. The Spirit and the bride say, 'Come.' Let each one who hears them say the same, 'Come.' Let the thirsty one come—anyone who wants to; let him come and drink the Water of Life without charge.

Jesus gives an invitation to everyone. For the Jews who are looking for their Messiah, He makes it plain, He is from the lineage of David - no need to look any further. For the Gentile who needs living water, come and drink without charge, He has already picked up the tab. What a wonderful invitation from the living Word of God. Will you "RSVP" by asking Jesus to forgive your insolence and come into your heart? Will you offer him your life without condition? That's what he did for you. I can't help but think that Jesus is giving us a hint of the spiritual circumstances when he returns. We've been reading about what events trigger his return in the physical world but I wonder...is he saying that this will be the event that triggers his return in the spiritual world? Is it when not only the Spirit (Holy Spirit) and the bride (those clothed in righteous acts) say "Come" but is it when everyone who hears them calling for him start saying the same thing? Is it when those thirsty for truth start saying "Come?" Is it when our constant prayer is "Thy Kingdom Come, Thy Will Be Done?" Is it when we say it and we really mean it? Is that when he will split the sky?

We know that you are a gentleman, Lord. You will not force your will on us...even if it means that most will choose death over life with you because they will not believe. But let me be one of the ones who joins the chant that hastens your return: "Come, Lord Jesus!"

The Book Of Revelation

IN ITS ENTIRETY

Revelation 1:1-20 KJV:

The Revelation of Jesus Christ, which God gave unto him, to shew unto his servants things which must shortly come to pass; and he sent and signified it by his angel unto his servant John: 2 Who bare record of the word of God, and of the testimony of Jesus Christ, and of all things that he saw. 3 Blessed is he that readeth, and they that hear the words of this prophecy, and keep those things which are written therein: for the time is at hand. 4 John to the seven churches which are in Asia: Grace be unto you, and peace, from him which is, and which was, and which is to come; and from the seven Spirits which are before his throne; 5 And from Jesus Christ, who is the faithful witness, and the first begotten of the dead, and the prince of the kings of the earth. Unto him that loved us, and washed us from our sins in his own blood, 6 And hath made us kings and priests unto God and his Father; to him be glory and dominion for ever and ever. Amen. 7 Behold, he cometh with clouds; and every eye shall see him, and they also which pierced him: and all kindreds of the earth shall wail because of him. Even so, Amen. 8 I am Alpha and Omega, the beginning and the ending, saith the Lord, which is, and which was, and which is to come, the Almighty. 9 I John,

*who also am your brother, and companion in tribulation, and in the
kingdom and patience of Jesus Christ, was in the isle that is called
Patmos, for the word of God, and for the testimony of Jesus Christ.
10 I was in the Spirit on the Lord's day, and heard behind me a
great voice, as of a trumpet, 11 Saying, I am Alpha and Omega,
the first and the last: and, What thou seest, write in a book, and
send it unto the seven churches which are in Asia; unto Ephesus,
and unto Smyrna, and unto Pergamos, and unto Thyatira, and unto
Sardis, and unto Philadelphia, and unto Laodicea. 12 And I turned
to see the voice that spake with me. And being turned, I saw seven
golden candlesticks; 13 And in the midst of the seven candlesticks
one like unto the Son of man, clothed with a garment down to the
foot, and girt about the paps with a golden girdle. 14 His head and
his hairs were white like wool, as white as snow; and his eyes were as
a flame of fire; 15 And his feet like unto fine brass, as if they burned
in a furnace; and his voice as the sound of many waters. 16 And
he had in his right hand seven stars: and out of his mouth went a
sharp two-edged sword: and his countenance was as the sun shineth
in his strength. 17 And when I saw him, I fell at his feet as dead.
And he laid his right hand upon me, saying unto me, Fear not; I am
the first and the last: 18 I am he that liveth, and was dead; and,
behold, I am alive for evermore, Amen; and have the keys of hell
and of death. 19 Write the things which thou hast seen, and the
things which are, and the things which shall be hereafter; 20 The
mystery of the seven stars which thou sawest in my right hand, and
the seven golden candlesticks. The seven stars are the angels of the
seven churches: and the seven candlesticks which thou sawest are
the seven churches.*

Revelation 2:1-28 KJV:

Unto the angel of the church of Ephesus write; These things saith

147

he that holdeth the seven stars in his right hand, who walketh in the midst of the seven golden candlesticks; 2 I know thy works, and thy labour, and thy patience, and how thou canst not bear them which are evil: and thou hast tried them which say they are apostles, and are not, and hast found them liars: 3 And hast borne, and hast patience, and for my name's sake hast laboured, and hast not fainted. 4 Nevertheless I have somewhat against thee, because thou hast left thy first love. 5 Remember therefore from whence thou art fallen, and repent, and do the first works; or else I will come unto thee quickly, and will remove thy candlestick out of his place, except thou repent. 6 But this thou hast, that thou hatest the deeds of the Nicolaitanes, which I also hate. 7 He that hath an ear, let him hear what the Spirit saith unto the churches; To him that overcometh will I give to eat of the tree of life, which is in the midst of the paradise of God. 8 And unto the angel of the church in Smyrna write; These things saith the first and the last, which was dead, and is alive; 9 I know thy works, and tribulation, and poverty, (but thou art rich) and I know the blasphemy of them which say they are Jews, and are not, but are the synagogue of Satan. 10 Fear none of those things which thou shalt suffer: behold, the devil shall cast some of you into prison, that ye may be tried; and ye shall have tribulation ten days: be thou faithful unto death, and I will give thee a crown of life. 11 He that hath an ear, let him hear what the Spirit saith unto the churches; He that overcometh shall not be hurt of the second death. 12 And to the angel of the church in Pergamos write; These things saith he which hath the sharp sword with two edges; 13 I know thy works, and where thou dwellest, even where Satan's seat is: and thou holdest fast my name, and hast not denied my faith, even in those days wherein Antipas was my faithful martyr, who was slain among you, where Satan dwelleth. 14 But I have a few things against thee, because thou hast there them that hold the doctrine of Balaam, who taught Balac to cast a stumblingblock before the children of Israel, to eat things sacrificed unto idols, and to commit fornication. 15 So hast thou also them that hold the doctrine of the Nicolaitanes, which thing I hate. 16 Repent; or else I will come unto thee quickly, and will fight against them with the sword of my mouth. 17 He that hath an ear, let him hear what the Spirit saith unto the churches; To him that overcometh will I give to eat of the hidden manna, and will give him a white stone, and in the stone a new name written, which no man knoweth saving he that receiveth it. 18 And unto the angel of the church in Thyatira write; These things saith the Son of God, who hath his eyes like unto a flame of fire, and his feet are like fine brass 19 I know thy works, and charity, and service, and faith, and thy patience, and thy works; and the last to be more than the first. 20 Notwithstanding I have a few things against thee, because thou sufferest that woman Jezebel, which calleth herself a prophetess, to teach and to seduce my servants to commit fornication, and to eat things sacrificed unto idols. 21 And I gave her space to repent of her fornication; and she repented not. 22 Behold, I will cast her into a bed, and them that commit adultery with her into great tribulation, except they repent of their deeds. 23 And I will kill her children with death; and all the churches shall know that I am he which searcheth the reins and hearts: and I will give unto every one of you according to your works. 24 But unto you I say, and unto the rest in Thyatira, as many as have not this doctrine, and which have not known the depths of Satan, as they speak; I will put upon you none other burden. 25 But that which ye have already hold fast till I come. 26 And he that overcometh, and keepeth my works unto the end, to him will I give power over the nations: 27 And he shall rule them with a rod of iron; as the vessels of a potter shall they be broken to shivers: even as I received of my Father. 28 And I will give him the morning star. 29 He that hath an ear, let him hear what the Spirit saith unto the churches.

Revelation 3:1-22 KJV:

And unto the angel of the church in Sardis write; These things saith he that hath the seven Spirits of God, and the seven stars; I know thy works, that thou hast a name that thou livest, and art dead. 2 Be watchful, and strengthen the things which remain, that are ready to die: for I have not found thy works perfect before God. 3 Remember therefore how thou hast received and heard, and hold fast, and repent. If therefore thou shalt not watch, I will come on thee as a thief, and thou shalt not know what hour I will come upon thee. 4 Thou hast a few names even in Sardis which have not defiled their garments; and they shall walk with me in white: for they are worthy. 5 He that overcometh, the same shall be clothed in white raiment; and I will not blot out his name out of the book of life, but I will confess his name before my Father, and before his angels. 6 He that hath an ear, let him hear what the Spirit saith unto the churches. 7 And to the angel of the church in Philadelphia write; These things saith he that is holy, he that is true, he that hath the key of David, he that openeth, and no man shutteth; and shutteth, and no man openeth; 8 I know thy works: behold, I have set before thee an open door, and no man can shut it: for thou hast a little strength, and hast kept my word, and hast not denied my name. 9 Behold, I will make them of the synagogue of Satan, which say they are Jews, and are not, but do lie; behold, I will make them to come and worship before thy feet, and to know that I have loved thee. 10 Because thou hast kept the word of my patience, I also will keep thee from the hour of temptation, which shall come upon all the world, to try them that dwell upon the earth. 11 Behold, I come quickly: hold that fast which thou hast, that no man take thy crown. 12 him that overcometh will I make a pillar in the temple of my God, and he shall go no more

150

out: and I will write upon him the name of my God, and the name of the city of my God, which is new Jerusalem, which cometh down out of heaven from my God: and I will write upon him my new name. 13 He that hath an ear, let him hear what the Spirit saith unto the churches. 14 And unto the angel of the church of the Laodiceans write; These things saith the Amen, the faithful and true witness, the beginning of the creation of God; 15 I know thy works, that thou art neither cold nor hot: I would thou wert cold or hot. 16 So then because thou art lukewarm, and neither cold nor hot, I will spue thee out of my mouth. 17 Because thou sayest, I am rich, and increased with goods, and have need of nothing; and knowest not that thou art wretched, and miserable, and poor, and blind, and naked: 18 I counsel thee to buy of me gold tried in the fire, that thou mayest be rich; and white raiment, that thou mayest be clothed, and that the shame of thy nakedness do not appear; and anoint thine eyes with eyesalve, that thou mayest see. 19 As many as I love, I rebuke and chasten: be zealous therefore, and repent. 20 Behold, I stand at the door, and knock: if any man hear my voice, and open the door, I will come in to him, and will sup with him, and he with me. 21 To him that overcometh will I grant to sit with me in my throne, even as I also overcame, and am set down with my Father in his throne. 22 He that hath an ear, let him hear what the Spirit saith unto the churches.

Revelation 4:1-11 KJV:

After this I looked, and, behold, a door was opened in heaven: and the first voice which I heard was as it were of a trumpet talking with me; which said, Come up hither, and I will shew thee things which must be hereafter. 2 And immediately I was in the spirit: and, behold, a throne was set in heaven, and one sat on the throne. 3 And he that sat was to look upon like a jasper and a sardine stone: and there was a rainbow round about the throne, in sight like unto an emerald. 4 And round about the throne were four and twenty seats: and upon the seats I saw four and twenty elders sitting, clothed in white raiment; and they had on their heads crowns of gold. 5 And out of the throne proceeded lightnings and thunderings and voices: and there were seven lamps of fire burning before the throne, which are the seven Spirits of God. 6 And before the throne there was a sea of glass like unto crystal: and in the midst of the throne, and round about the throne, were four beasts full of eyes before and behind. 7 And the first beast was like a lion, and the second beast like a calf, and the third beast had a face as a man, and the fourth beast was like a flying eagle. 8 And the four beasts had each of them six wings about him; and they were full of eyes within: and they rest not day and night, saying, Holy, holy, holy, Lord God Almighty, which was, and is, and is to come. 9 And when those beasts give glory and honour and thanks to him that sat on the throne, who liveth for ever and ever, 10 The four and twenty elders fall down before him that sat on the throne, and worship him that liveth for ever and ever, and cast their crowns before the throne, saying, 11 Thou art worthy, O Lord, to receive glory and honour and power: for thou hast created all things, and for thy pleasure they are and were created.

Revelation 5:1-14 KJV:

And I saw in the right hand of him that sat on the throne a book written within and on the backside, sealed with seven seals. 2 And I saw a strong angel proclaiming with a loud voice, Who is worthy to open the book, and to loose the seals thereof? 3 And no man in heaven, nor in earth, neither under the earth, was able to open the book, neither to look thereon. 4 And I wept much, because no man was found worthy to open and to read the book, neither to look thereon. 5 And one of the elders saith unto me, Weep not: behold, the

*Lion of the tribe of Judah, the Root of David, hath prevailed to open the book, and to loose the seven seals thereof. **6** And I beheld, and, lo, in the midst of the throne and of the four beasts, and in the midst of the elders, stood a Lamb as it had been slain, having seven horns and seven eyes, which are the seven Spirits of God sent forth into all the earth. **7** And he came and took the book out of the right hand of him that sat upon the throne. **8** And when he had taken the book, the four beasts and four and twenty elders fell down before the Lamb, having every one of them harps, and golden vials full of odours, which are the prayers of saints. **9** And they sung a new song, saying, Thou art worthy to take the book, and to open the seals thereof: for thou wast slain, and hast redeemed us to God by thy blood out of every kindred, and tongue, and people, and nation; **10** And hast made us unto our God kings and priests: and we shall reign on the earth. **11** And I beheld, and I heard the voice of many angels round about the throne and the beasts and the elders: and the number of them was ten thousand times ten thousand, and thousands of thousands; **12** Saying with a loud voice, Worthy is the Lamb that was slain to receive power, and riches, and wisdom, and strength, and honour, and glory, and blessing. **13** And every creature which is in heaven, and on the earth, and under the earth, and such as are in the sea, and all that are in them, heard I saying, Blessing, and honour, and glory, and power, be unto him that sitteth upon the throne, and unto the Lamb for ever and ever. **14** And the four beasts said, Amen. And the four and twenty elders fell down and worshipped him that liveth for ever and ever.*

Revelation 6:1-17 KJV:

*And I saw when the Lamb opened one of the seals, and I heard, as it were the noise of thunder, one of the four beasts saying, Come and see. **2** And I saw, and behold a white horse: and he that sat on*

153

him had a bow; and a crown was given unto him: and he went forth conquering, and to conquer. 3 And when he had opened the second seal, I heard the second beast say, Come and see. 4 And there went out another horse that was red: and power was given to him that sat thereon to take peace from the earth, and that they should kill one another: and there was given unto him a great sword. 5 And when he had opened the third seal, I heard the third beast say, Come and see. And I beheld, and lo a black horse; and he that sat on him had a pair of balances in his hand. 6 And I heard a voice in the midst of the four beasts say, A measure of wheat for a penny, and three measures of barley for a penny; and see thou hurt not the oil and the wine. 7 And when he had opened the fourth seal, I heard the voice of the fourth beast say, Come and see. 8 And I looked, and behold a pale horse: and his name that sat on him was Death, and Hell followed with him. And power was given unto them over the fourth part of the earth, to kill with sword, and with hunger, and with death, and with the beasts of the earth. 9 And when he had opened the fifth seal, I saw under the altar the souls of them that were slain for the word of God, and for the testimony which they held: 10 And they cried with a loud voice, saying, How long, O Lord, holy and true, dost thou not judge and avenge our blood on them that dwell on the earth? 11 And white robes were given unto every one of them; and it was said unto them, that they should rest yet for a little season, until their fellowservants also and their brethren, that should be killed as they were, should be fulfilled. 12 And I beheld when he had opened the sixth seal, and, lo, there was a great earthquake; and the sun became black as sackcloth of hair, and the moon became as blood; 13 And the stars of heaven fell unto the earth, even as a fig tree casteth her untimely figs, when she is shaken of a mighty wind. 14 And the heaven departed as a scroll when it is rolled together; and every mountain and island were moved out of their places. 15

And the kings of the earth, and the great men, and the rich men, and the chief captains, and the mighty men, and every bondman, and every free man, hid themselves in the dens and in the rocks of the mountains; 16 And said to the mountains and rocks, Fall on us, and hide us from the face of him that sitteth on the throne, and from the wrath of the Lamb: 17 For the great day of his wrath is come; and who shall be able to stand?

Revelation 7:1-17 KJV:

And after these things I saw four angels standing on the four corners of the earth, holding the four winds of the earth, that the wind should not blow on the earth, nor on the sea, nor on any tree. 2 And I saw another angel ascending from the east, having the seal of the living God: and he cried with a loud voice to the four angels, to whom it was given to hurt the earth and the sea, 3 Saying, Hurt not the earth, neither the sea, nor the trees, till we have sealed the servants of our God in their foreheads. 4 And I heard the number of them which were sealed: and there were sealed an hundred and forty and four thousand of all the tribes of the children of Israel. 5 Of the tribe of Juda were sealed twelve thousand. Of the tribe of Reuben were sealed twelve thousand. Of the tribe of Gad were sealed twelve thousand. 6 Of the tribe of Aser were sealed twelve thousand. Of the tribe of Nephthalim were sealed twelve thousand. Of the tribe of Manasses were sealed twelve thousand. 7 Of the tribe of Simeon were sealed twelve thousand. Of the tribe of Levi were sealed twelve thousand. Of the tribe of Issachar were sealed twelve thousand. 8 Of the tribe of Zabulon were sealed twelve thousand. Of the tribe of Joseph were sealed twelve thousand. Of the tribe of Benjamin were sealed twelve thousand. 9 After this I beheld, and, lo, a great multitude, which no man could number, of all nations, and kindreds, and people, and tongues, stood before the throne, and before the Lamb, clothed with white robes, and palms in their hands; 10 And cried with a loud voice, saying, Salvation to our God which sitteth upon the throne, and unto the Lamb. 11 And all the angels stood round about the throne, and about the elders and the four beasts, and fell before the throne on their faces, and worshipped God, 12 Saying, Amen: Blessing, and glory, and wisdom, and thanksgiving, and honour, and power, and might, be unto our God for ever and ever Amen. 13 And one of the elders answered, saying unto me, What are these which are arrayed in white robes? and whence came they? 14 And I said unto him, Sir, thou knowest. And he said to me, These are they which came out of great tribulation, and have washed their robes, and made them white in the blood of the Lamb. 15 Therefore are they before the throne of God, and serve him day and night in his temple: and he that sitteth on the throne shall dwell among them. 16 They shall hunger no more, neither thirst any more; neither shall the sun light on them, nor any heat. 17 For the Lamb which is in the midst of the throne shall feed them, and shall lead them unto living fountains of waters: and God shall wipe away all tears from their eyes.

Revelation 8:1-13 KJV:

And when he had opened the seventh seal, there was silence in heaven about the space of half an hour. 2 And I saw the seven angels which stood before God; and to them were given seven trumpets. 3 And another angel came and stood at the altar, having a golden censer; and there was given unto him much incense, that he should offer it with the prayers of all saints upon the golden altar which was before the throne. 4 And the smoke of the incense, which came with the prayers of the saints, ascended up before God out of the angel's hand. 5 And the angel took the censer, and filled it with fire of the altar, and cast it into the earth: and there were voices, and thunderings, and lightnings, and an earthquake. 6 And the seven

156

angels which had the seven trumpets prepared themselves to sound. *7 The first angel sounded, and there followed hail and fire mingled with blood, and they were cast upon the earth: and the third part of trees was burnt up, and all green grass was burnt up. 8 And the second angel sounded, and as it were a great mountain burning with fire was cast into the sea: and the third part of the sea became blood; 9 And the third part of the creatures which were in the sea, and had life, died; and the third part of the ships were destroyed. 10 And the third angel sounded, and there fell a great star from heaven, burning as it were a lamp, and it fell upon the third part of the rivers, and upon the fountains of waters; 11 And the name of the star is called Wormwood: and the third part of the waters became wormwood; and many men died of the waters, because they were made bitter. 12 And the fourth angel sounded, and the third part of the sun was smitten, and the third part of the moon, and the third part of the stars; so as the third part of them was darkened, and the day shone not for a third part of it, and the night likewise. 13 And I beheld, and heard an angel flying through the midst of heaven, saying with a loud voice, Woe, woe, woe, to the inhabiters of the earth by reason of the other voices of the trumpet of the three angels, which are yet to sound!*

Revelation 9:1-21 KJV:

And the fifth angel sounded, and I saw a star fall from heaven unto the earth: and to him was given the key of the bottomless pit. 2 And he opened the bottomless pit; and there arose a smoke out of the pit, as the smoke of a great furnace; and the sun and the air were darkened by reason of the smoke of the pit. 3 And there came out of the smoke locusts upon the earth: and unto them was given power, as the scorpions of the earth have power. 4 And it was commanded them that they should not hurt the grass of the earth, neither any green thing, neither any tree; but only those men which have not the seal of God in their foreheads. 5 And to them it was given that they should not kill them, but that they should be tormented five months: and their torment was as the torment of a scorpion, when he striketh a man. 6 And in those days shall men seek death, and shall not find it; and shall desire to die, and death shall flee from them. 7 And the shapes of the locusts were like unto horses prepared unto battle; and on their heads were as it were crowns like gold, and their faces were as the faces of men. 8 And they had hair as the hair of women, and their teeth were as the teeth of lions. 9 And they had breastplates, as it were breastplates of iron; and the sound of their wings was as the sound of chariots of many horses running to battle. 10 And they had tails like unto scorpions, and there were stings in their tails: and their power was to hurt men five months. 11 And they had a king over them, which is the angel of the bottomless pit, whose name in the Hebrew tongue is Abaddon, but in the Greek tongue hath his name Apollyon. 12 One woe is past; and, behold, there come two woes more hereafter. 13 And the sixth angel sounded, and I heard a voice from the four horns of the golden altar which is before God, 14 Saying to the sixth angel which had the trumpet, Loose the four angels which are bound in the great river Euphrates. 15 And the four angels were loosed, which were prepared for an hour, and a day, and a month, and a year, for to slay the third part of men. 16 And the number of the army of the horsemen were two hundred thousand thousand: and I heard the number of them. 17 And thus I saw the horses in the vision, and them that sat on them, having breastplates of fire, and of jacinth, and brimstone: and the heads of the horses were as the heads of lions; and out of their mouths issued fire and smoke and brimstone. 18 By these three was the third part of men killed, by the fire, and by the smoke, and by the brimstone, which issued out of their mouths. 19 For their power is in their mouth, and in their tails: for their tails were like unto serpents, and had

158

*heads, and with them they do hurt. **20** And the rest of the men which were not killed by these plagues yet repented not of the works of their hands, that they should not worship devils, and idols of gold, and silver, and brass, and stone, and of wood: which neither can see, nor hear, nor walk: **21** Neither repented they of their murders, nor of their sorceries, nor of their fornication, nor of their thefts.*

Revelation 10:1-11 KJV:

*And I saw another mighty angel come down from heaven, clothed with a cloud: and a rainbow was upon his head, and his face was as it were the sun, and his feet as pillars of fire: **2** And he had in his hand a little book open: and he set his right foot upon the sea, and his left foot on the earth, **3** And cried with a loud voice, as when a lion roareth: and when he had cried, seven thunders uttered their voices. **4** And when the seven thunders had uttered their voices, I was about to write: and I heard a voice from heaven saying unto me, Seal up those things which the seven thunders uttered, and write them not. **5** And the angel which I saw stand upon the sea and upon the earth lifted up his hand to heaven, **6** And sware by him that liveth for ever and ever, who created heaven, and the things that therein are, and the earth, and the things that therein are, and the sea, and the things which are therein, that there should be time no longer: **7** But in the days of the voice of the seventh angel, when he shall begin to sound, the mystery of God should be finished, as he hath declared to his servants the prophets. **8** And the voice which I heard from heaven spake unto me again, and said, Go and take the little book which is open in the hand of the angel which standeth upon the sea and upon the earth. **9** And I went unto the angel, and said unto him, Give me the little book. And he said unto me, Take it, and eat it up; and it shall make thy belly bitter, but it shall be in thy mouth sweet as honey. **10** And I took the little book out of the angel's hand, and ate*

159

it up; and it was in my mouth sweet as honey: and as soon as I had eaten it, my belly was bitter. **11** *And he said unto me, Thou must prophesy again before many peoples, and nations, and tongues, and kings.*

Revelation 11:1-19 KJV:

And there was given me a reed like unto a rod: and the angel stood, saying, Rise, and measure the temple of God, and the altar, and them that worship therein. **2** *But the court which is without the temple leave out, and measure it not; for it is given unto the Gentiles: and the holy city shall they tread under foot forty and two months.* **3** *And I will give power unto my two witnesses, and they shall prophesy a thousand two hundred and threescore days, clothed in sackcloth.* **4** *These are the two olive trees, and the two candlesticks standing before the God of the earth.* **5** *And if any man will hurt them, fire proceedeth out of their mouth, and devoureth their enemies: and if any man will hurt them, he must in this manner be killed.* **6** *These have power to shut heaven, that it rain not in the days of their prophecy: and have power over waters to turn them to blood, and to smite the earth with all plagues, as often as they will.* **7** *And when they shall have finished their testimony, the beast that ascendeth out of the bottomless pit shall make war against them, and shall overcome them, and kill them.* **8** *And their dead bodies shall lie in the street of the great city, which spiritually is called Sodom and Egypt, where also our Lord was crucified.* **9** *And they of the people and kindreds and tongues and nations shall see their dead bodies three days and an half, and shall not suffer their dead bodies to be put in graves.* **10** *And they that dwell upon the earth shall rejoice over them, and make merry, and shall send gifts one to another; because these two prophets tormented them that dwelt on the earth.* **11** *And after three days and an half the spirit of life from God entered into* them, and they stood upon their feet; and great fear fell upon them which saw them. *12 And they heard a great voice from heaven saying unto them, Come up hither. And they ascended up to heaven in a cloud; and their enemies beheld them. 13 And the same hour was there a great earthquake, and the tenth part of the city fell, and in the earthquake were slain of men seven thousand: and the remnant were affrighted, and gave glory to the God of heaven. 14 The second woe is past; and, behold, the third woe cometh quickly. 15 And the seventh angel sounded; and there were great voices in heaven, saying, The kingdoms of this world are become the kingdoms of our Lord, and of his Christ; and he shall reign for ever and ever. 16 And the four and twenty elders, which sat before God on their seats, fell upon their faces, and worshipped God, 17 Saying, We give thee thanks, O Lord God Almighty, which art, and wast, and art to come; because thou hast taken to thee thy great power, and hast reigned. 18 And the nations were angry, and thy wrath is come, and the time of the dead, that they should be judged, and that thou shouldest give reward unto thy servants the prophets, and to the saints, and them that fear thy name, small and great; and shouldest destroy them which destroy the earth. 19 And the temple of God was opened in heaven, and there was seen in his temple the ark of his testament: and there were lightnings, and voices, and thunderings, and an earthquake, and great hail.*

Revelation 12:1-17 KJV:

And there appeared a great wonder in heaven; a woman clothed with the sun, and the moon under her feet, and upon her head a crown of twelve stars: 2 And she being with child cried, travailing in birth, and pained to be delivered. 3 And there appeared another wonder in heaven; and behold a great red dragon, having seven heads and ten horns, and seven crowns upon his heads. 4 And his tail drew the

161

third part of the stars of heaven, and did cast them to the earth: and the dragon stood before the woman which was ready to be delivered, for to devour her child as soon as it was born. 5 And she brought forth a man child, who was to rule all nations with a rod of iron: and her child was caught up unto God, and to his throne. 6 And the woman fled into the wilderness, where she hath a place prepared of God, that they should feed her there a thousand two hundred and threescore days. 7 And there was war in heaven: Michael and his angels fought against the dragon; and the dragon fought and his angels, 8 And prevailed not; neither was their place found any more in heaven. 9 And the great dragon was cast out, that old serpent, called the Devil, and Satan, which deceiveth the whole world: he was cast out into the earth, and his angels were cast out with him. 10 And I heard a loud voice saying in heaven, Now is come salvation, and strength, and the kingdom of our God, and the power of his Christ: for the accuser of our brethren is cast down, which accused them before our God day and night. 11 And they overcame him by the blood of the Lamb, and by the word of their testimony; and they loved not their lives unto the death. 12 Therefore rejoice, ye heavens, and ye that dwell in them. Woe to the inhabiters of the earth and of the sea! for the devil is come down unto you, having great wrath, because he knoweth that he hath but a short time. 13 And when the dragon saw that he was cast unto the earth, he persecuted the woman which brought forth the man child. 14 And to the woman were given two wings of a great eagle, that she might fly into the wilderness, into her place, where she is nourished for a time, and times, and half a time, from the face of the serpent. 15 And the serpent cast out of his mouth water as a flood after the woman, that he might cause her to be carried away of the flood. 16 And the earth helped the woman, and the earth opened her mouth, and swallowed up the flood which the dragon cast out of his mouth. 17 And the dragon was wroth with the woman, and went to make war with the remnant of her seed, which keep the commandments of God, and have the testimony of Jesus Christ.

Revelation 13:1-18 KJV:

And I stood upon the sand of the sea, and saw a beast rise up out of the sea, having seven heads and ten horns, and upon his horns ten crowns, and upon his heads the name of blasphemy. 2 And the beast which I saw was like unto a leopard, and his feet were as the feet of a bear, and his mouth as the mouth of a lion: and the dragon gave him his power, and his seat, and great authority. 3 And I saw one of his heads as it were wounded to death; and his deadly wound was healed: and all the world wondered after the beast. 4 And they worshipped the dragon which gave power unto the beast: and they worshipped the beast, saying, Who is like unto the beast? who is able to make war with him? 5 And there was given unto him a mouth speaking great things and blasphemies; and power was given unto him to continue forty and two months. 6 And he opened his mouth in blasphemy against God, to blaspheme his name, and his tabernacle, and them that dwell in heaven. 7 And it was given unto him to make war with the saints, and to overcome them: and power was given him over all kindreds, and tongues, and nations. 8 And all that dwell upon the earth shall worship him, whose names are not written in the book of life of the Lamb slain from the foundation of the world. 9 If any man have an ear, let him hear. 10 He that leadeth into captivity shall go into captivity: he that killeth with the sword must be killed with the sword. Here is the patience and the faith of the saints. 11 And I beheld another beast coming up out of the earth; and he had two horns like a lamb, and he spake as a dragon. 12 And he exerciseth all the power of the first beast before him, and causeth the earth and them which dwell therein to worship the first beast, whose deadly wound was healed. 13 And he doeth great wonders, so that he maketh fire come down from heaven on the earth in the sight of men, 14 And deceiveth them that dwell on the earth by the means of those miracles which he had power to do in the sight of the beast; saying to them that dwell on the earth, that they should make an image to the beast, which had the wound by a sword, and did live. 15 And he had power to give life unto the image of the beast, that the image of the beast should both speak, and cause that as many as would not worship the image of the beast should be killed. 16 And he causeth all, both small and great, rich and poor, free and bond, to receive a mark in their right hand, or in their foreheads: 17 And that no man might buy or sell, save he that had the mark, or the name of the beast, or the number of his name. 18 Here is wisdom. Let him that hath understanding count the number of the beast: for it is the number of a man; and his number is Six hundred threescore and six.

Revelation 14:1-20 KJV:

And I looked, and, lo, a Lamb stood on the mount Sion, and with him an hundred forty and four thousand, having his Father's name written in their foreheads. 2 And I heard a voice from heaven, as the voice of many waters, and as the voice of a great thunder: and I heard the voice of harpers harping with their harps: 3 And they sung as it were a new song before the throne, and before the four beasts, and the elders: and no man could learn that song but the hundred and forty and four thousand, which were redeemed from the earth. 4 These are they which were not defiled with women; for they are virgins. These are they which follow the Lamb whithersoever he goeth. These were redeemed from among men, being the firstfruits unto God and to the Lamb. 5 And in their mouth was found no guile: for they are without fault before the throne of God. 6 And I saw another angel fly in the midst of heaven, having the everlasting gospel to preach unto them that dwell on the earth, and to every nation, and kindred, and tongue, and people, 7 Saying with a loud voice, Fear God, and give glory to him; for the hour of his judgment is come: and worship him that made heaven, and earth, and the sea, and the fountains of waters. 8 And there followed another angel, saying, Babylon is fallen, is fallen, that great city, because she made all nations drink of the wine of the wrath of her fornication. 9 And the third angel followed them, saying with a loud voice, If any man worship the beast and his image, and receive his mark in his forehead, or in his hand, 10 The same shall drink of the wine of the wrath of God, which is poured out without mixture into the cup of his indignation; and he shall be tormented with fire and brimstone in the presence of the holy angels, and in the presence of the Lamb: 11 And the smoke of their torment ascendeth up for ever and ever: and they have no rest day nor night, who worship the beast and his image, and whosoever receiveth the mark of his name. 12 Here is the patience of the saints: here are they that keep the commandments of God, and the faith of Jesus. 13 And I heard a voice from heaven saying unto me, Write, Blessed are the dead which die in the Lord from henceforth: Yea, saith the Spirit, that they may rest from their labours; and their works do follow them. 14 And I looked, and behold a white cloud, and upon the cloud one sat like unto the Son of man, having on his head a golden crown, and in his hand a sharp sickle. 15 And another angel came out of the temple, crying with a loud voice to him that sat on the cloud, Thrust in thy sickle, and reap: for the time is come for thee to reap; for the harvest of the earth is ripe. 16 And he that sat on the cloud thrust in his sickle on the earth; and the earth was reaped. 17 And another angel came out of the temple which is in heaven, he also having a sharp sickle. 18 And another angel came out from the altar, which had power over fire; and cried with a loud cry to him that had

165

the sharp sickle, saying, Thrust in thy sharp sickle, and gather the clusters of the vine of the earth; for her grapes are fully ripe. 19 And the angel thrust in his sickle into the earth, and gathered the vine of the earth, and cast it into the great winepress of the wrath of God. 20 And the winepress was trodden without the city, and blood came out of the winepress, even unto the horse bridles, by the space of a thousand and six hundred furlongs.

Revelation 15:1-8 KJV:

And I saw another sign in heaven, great and marvellous, seven angels having the seven last plagues; for in them is filled up the wrath of God. 2 And I saw as it were a sea of glass mingled with fire: and them that had gotten the victory over the beast, and over his image, and over his mark, and over the number of his name, stand on the sea of glass, having the harps of God. 3 And they sing the song of Moses the servant of God, and the song of the Lamb, saying, Great and marvellous are thy works, Lord God Almighty; just and true are thy ways, thou King of saints. 4 Who shall not fear thee, O Lord, and glorify thy name? for thou only art holy: for all nations shall come and worship before thee; for thy judgments are made manifest. 5 And after that I looked, and, behold, the temple of the tabernacle of the testimony in heaven was opened: 6 And the seven angels came out of the temple, having the seven plagues, clothed in pure and white linen, and having their breasts girded with golden girdles. 7 And one of the four beasts gave unto the seven angels seven golden vials full of the wrath of God, who liveth for ever and ever. 8 And the temple was filled with smoke from the glory of God, and from his power; and no man was able to enter into the temple, till the seven plagues of the seven angels were fulfilled.

Revelation 16:1-21 KJV:

And I heard a great voice out of the temple saying to the seven angels, Go your ways, and pour out the vials of the wrath of God upon the earth. 2 *And the first went, and poured out his vial upon the earth; and there fell a noisome and grievous sore upon the men which had the mark of the beast, and upon them which worshipped his image.* 3 *And the second angel poured out his vial upon the sea; and it became as the blood of a dead man: and every living soul died in the sea.* 4 *And the third angel poured out his vial upon the rivers and fountains of waters; and they became blood.* 5 *And I heard the angel of the waters say, Thou art righteous, O Lord, which art, and wast, and shalt be, because thou hast judged thus.* 6 *For they have shed the blood of saints and prophets, and thou hast given them blood to drink; for they are worthy.* 7 *And I heard another out of the altar say, Even so, Lord God Almighty, true and righteous are thy judgments.* 8 *And the fourth angel poured out his vial upon the sun; and power was given unto him to scorch men with fire.* 9 *And men were scorched with great heat, and blasphemed the name of God, which hath power over these plagues: and they repented not to give him glory.* 10 *And the fifth angel poured out his vial upon the seat of the beast; and his kingdom was full of darkness; and they gnawed their tongues for pain,* 11 *And blasphemed the God of heaven because of their pains and their sores, and repented not of their deeds.* 12 *And the sixth angel poured out his vial upon the great river Euphrates; and the water thereof was dried up, that the way of the kings of the east might be prepared.* 13 *And I saw three unclean spirits like frogs come out of the mouth of the dragon, and out of the mouth of the beast, and out of the mouth of the false prophet.* 14 *For they are the spirits of devils, working miracles, which go forth unto the kings of the earth and of the whole world, to gather them to the battle of that great day of God Almighty.* 15 *Behold, I come as a thief. Blessed is he that watcheth, and keepeth his garments, lest he walk naked,*

167

and they see his shame. **16** *And he gathered them together into a place called in the Hebrew tongue Armageddon.* **17** *And the seventh angel poured out his vial into the air; and there came a great voice out of the temple of heaven, from the throne, saying, It is done.* **18** *And there were voices, and thunders, and lightnings; and there was a great earthquake, such as was not since men were upon the earth, so mighty an earthquake, and so great.* **19** *And the great city was divided into three parts, and the cities of the nations fell: and great Babylon came in remembrance before God, to give unto her the cup of the wine of the fierceness of his wrath.* **20** *And every island fled away, and the mountains were not found.* **21** *And there fell upon men a great hail out of heaven, every stone about the weight of a talent: and men blasphemed God because of the plague of the hail; for the plague thereof was exceeding great.*

Revelation 17:1-18 KJV:

And there came one of the seven angels which had the seven vials, and talked with me, saying unto me, Come hither; I will shew unto thee the judgment of the great whore that sitteth upon many waters: **2** *With whom the kings of the earth have committed fornication, and the inhabitants of the earth have been made drunk with the wine of her fornication.* **3** *So he carried me away in the spirit into the wilderness: and I saw a woman sit upon a scarlet coloured beast, full of names of blasphemy, having seven heads and ten horns.* **4** *And the woman was arrayed in purple and scarlet colour, and decked with gold and precious stones and pearls, having a golden cup in her hand full of abominations and filthiness of her fornication:* **5** *And upon her forehead was a name written, Mystery, Babylon The Great, The Mother Of Harlots And Abominations Of The earth.* **6** *And I saw the woman drunken with the blood of the saints, and with the blood of the martyrs of Jesus: and when I saw her, I wondered with* *great admiration. 7 And the angel said unto me, Wherefore didst thou marvel? I will tell thee the mystery of the woman, and of the beast that carrieth her, which hath the seven heads and ten horns. 8 The beast that thou sawest was, and is not; and shall ascend out of the bottomless pit, and go into perdition: and they that dwell on the earth shall wonder, whose names were not written in the book of life from the foundation of the world, when they behold the beast that was, and is not, and yet is. 9 And here is the mind which hath wisdom. The seven heads are seven mountains, on which the woman sitteth. 10 And there are seven kings: five are fallen, and one is, and the other is not yet come; and when he cometh, he must continue a short space. 11 And the beast that was, and is not, even he is the eighth, and is of the seven, and goeth into perdition. 12 And the ten horns which thou sawest are ten kings, which have received no kingdom as yet; but receive power as kings one hour with the beast. 13 These have one mind, and shall give their power and strength unto the beast. 14 These shall make war with the Lamb, and the Lamb shall overcome them: for he is Lord of lords, and King of kings: and they that are with him are called, and chosen, and faithful. 15 And he saith unto me, The waters which thou sawest, where the whore sitteth, are peoples, and multitudes, and nations, and tongues. 16 And the ten horns which thou sawest upon the beast, these shall hate the whore, and shall make her desolate and naked, and shall eat her flesh, and burn her with fire. 17 For God hath put in their hearts to fulfil his will, and to agree, and give their kingdom unto the beast, until the words of God shall be fulfilled. 18 And the woman which thou sawest is that great city, which reigneth over the kings of the earth.*

Revelation 18:1-24 KJV:

And after these things I saw another angel come down from heaven, having great power; and the earth was lightened with his glory. 2 And he cried mightily with a strong voice, saying, Babylon the great is fallen, is fallen, and is become the habitation of devils, and the hold of every foul spirit, and a cage of every unclean and hateful bird. 3 For all nations have drunk of the wine of the wrath of her fornication, and the kings of the earth have committed fornication with her, and the merchants of the earth are waxed rich through the abundance of her delicacies. 4 And I heard another voice from heaven, saying, Come out of her, my people, that ye be not partakers of her sins, and that ye receive not of her plagues. 5 For her sins have reached unto heaven, and God hath remembered her iniquities. 6 Reward her even as she rewarded you, and double unto her double according to her works: in the cup which she hath filled fill to her double. 7 How much she hath glorified herself, and lived deliciously, so much torment and sorrow give her: for she saith in her heart, I sit a queen, and am no widow, and shall see no sorrow. 8 Therefore shall her plagues come in one day, death, and mourning, and famine; and she shall be utterly burned with fire: for strong is the Lord God who judgeth her. 9 And the kings of the earth, who have committed fornication and lived deliciously with her, shall bewail her, and lament for her, when they shall see the smoke of her burning, 10 Standing afar off for the fear of her torment, saying, Alas, alas that great city Babylon, that mighty city! for in one hour is thy judgment come. 11 And the merchants of the earth shall weep and mourn over her; for no man buyeth their merchandise any more: 12 The merchandise of gold, and silver, and precious stones, and of pearls, and fine linen, and purple, and silk, and scarlet, and all thyine wood, and all manner vessels of ivory, and all manner vessels of most precious wood, and of brass, and iron, and marble, 13 And cinnamon, and odours, and ointments, and frankincense, and wine, and oil, and fine flour, and wheat, and beasts, and sheep, and horses, and chariots, and slaves, and souls of men. 14 And the fruits that thy soul lusted after are departed from thee, and all things which were dainty and are departed from thee, and thou shalt find them no more at all. 15 The merchants of these things, which were made rich by her, shall stand afar off for the fear of her torment, weeping and wailing, 16 And saying, Alas, alas that great city, that was clothed in fine linen, and purple, and scarlet, and decked with gold, and precious stones, and pearls! 17 For in one hour so great riches is come to nought. And every shipmaster, and all the company in ships, and sailors, and as many as trade by sea, stood afar off, 18 And cried when they saw the smoke of her burning, saying, What city is like unto this great city! 19 And they cast dust on their heads, and cried, weeping and wailing, saying, Alas, alas that great city, wherein were made rich all that had ships in the sea by reason of her costliness! for in one hour is she made desolate. 20 Rejoice over her, thou heaven, and ye holy apostles and prophets; for God hath avenged you on her. 21 And a mighty angel took up a stone like a great millstone, and cast it into the sea, saying, Thus with violence shall that great city Babylon be thrown down, and shall be found no more at all. 22 And the voice of harpers, and musicians, and of pipers, and trumpeters, shall be heard no more at all in thee; and no craftsman, of whatsoever craft he be, shall be found any more in thee; and the sound of a millstone shall be heard no more at all in thee; 23 And the light of a candle shall shine no more at all in thee; and the voice of the bridegroom and of the bride shall be heard no more at all in thee: for thy merchants were the great men of the earth; for by thy sorceries were all nations deceived. 24 And in her was found the blood of prophets, and of saints, and of all that were slain upon the earth.

Revelation 19:1-21 KJV:

And after these things I heard a great voice of much people in

171

heaven, saying, Alleluia; Salvation, and glory, and honour, and power, unto the Lord our God: 2 For true and righteous are his judgments: for he hath judged the great whore, which did corrupt the earth with her fornication, and hath avenged the blood of his servants at her hand. 3 And again they said, Alleluia And her smoke rose up for ever and ever. 4 And the four and twenty elders and the four beasts fell down and worshipped God that sat on the throne, saying, Amen; Alleluia. 5 And a voice came out of the throne, saying, Praise our God, all ye his servants, and ye that fear him, both small and great. 6 And I heard as it were the voice of a great multitude, and as the voice of many waters, and as the voice of mighty thunderings, saying, Alleluia: for the Lord God omnipotent reigneth. 7 Let us be glad and rejoice, and give honour to him: for the marriage of the Lamb is come, and his wife hath made herself ready. 8 And to her was granted that she should be arrayed in fine linen, clean and white: for the fine linen is the righteousness of saints. 9 And he saith unto me, Write, Blessed are they which are called unto the marriage supper of the Lamb. And he saith unto me, These are the true sayings of God. 10 And I fell at his feet to worship him. And he said unto me, See thou do it not: I am thy fellowservant, and of thy brethren that have the testimony of Jesus: worship God: for the testimony of Jesus is the spirit of prophecy. 11 And I saw heaven opened, and behold a white horse; and he that sat upon him was called Faithful and True, and in righteousness he doth judge and make war. 12 His eyes were as a flame of fire, and on his head were many crowns; and he had a name written, that no man knew, but he himself. 13 And he was clothed with a vesture dipped in blood: and his name is called The Word of God. 14 And the armies which were in heaven followed him upon white horses, clothed in fine linen, white and clean. 15 And out of his mouth goeth a sharp sword, that with it he should smite the nations: and he shall rule them with a rod of iron: and he

172

*treadeth the winepress of the fierceness and wrath of Almighty God.
16 And he hath on his vesture and on his thigh a name written, King
Of Kings, And Lord Of Lords. 17 And I saw an angel standing in
the sun; and he cried with a loud voice, saying to all the fowls that
fly in the midst of heaven, Come and gather yourselves together unto
the supper of the great God; 18 That ye may eat the flesh of kings,
and the flesh of captains, and the flesh of mighty men, and the flesh
of horses, and of them that sit on them, and the flesh of all men, both
free and bond, both small and great. 19 And I saw the beast, and
the kings of the earth, and their armies, gathered together to make
war against him that sat on the horse, and against his army. 20 And
the beast was taken, and with him the false prophet that wrought
miracles before him, with which he deceived them that had received
the mark of the beast, and them that worshipped his image. These
both were cast alive into a lake of fire burning with brimstone. 21
And the remnant were slain with the sword of him that sat upon the
horse, which sword proceeded out of his mouth: and all the fowls
were filled with their flesh.*

Revelation 20:1-15 KJV:

*And I saw an angel come down from heaven, having the key of
the bottomless pit and a great chain in his hand. 2 And he laid hold
on the dragon, that old serpent, which is the Devil, and Satan, and
bound him a thousand years, 3 And cast him into the bottomless pit,
and shut him up, and set a seal upon him, that he should deceive the
nations no more, till the thousand years should be fulfilled: and after
that he must be loosed a little season. 4 And I saw thrones, and they
sat upon them, and judgment was given unto them: and I saw the
souls of them that were beheaded for the witness of Jesus, and for the
word of God, and which had not worshipped the beast, neither his
image, neither had received his mark upon their foreheads, or in their*

173

hands; and they lived and reigned with Christ a thousand years. 5 But the rest of the dead lived not again until the thousand years were finished. This is the first resurrection. 6 Blessed and holy is he that hath part in the first resurrection: on such the second death hath no power, but they shall be priests of God and of Christ, and shall reign with him a thousand years. 7 And when the thousand years are expired, Satan shall be loosed out of his prison, 8 And shall go out to deceive the nations which are in the four quarters of the earth, Gog, and Magog, to gather them together to battle: the number of whom is as the sand of the sea. 9 And they went up on the breadth of the earth, and compassed the camp of the saints about, and the beloved city: and fire came down from God out of heaven, and devoured them. 10 And the devil that deceived them was cast into the lake of fire and brimstone, where the beast and the false prophet are, and shall be tormented day and night for ever and ever. 11 And I saw a great white throne, and him that sat on it, from whose face the earth and the heaven fled away; and there was found no place for them. 12 And I saw the dead, small and great, stand before God; and the books were opened: and another book was opened, which is the book of life: and the dead were judged out of those things which were written in the books, according to their works. 13 And the sea gave up the dead which were in it; and death and hell delivered up the dead which were in them: and they were judged every man according to their works. 14 And death and hell were cast into the lake of fire. This is the second death. 15 And whosoever was not found written in the book of life was cast into the lake of fire.

Revelation 21:1-27 KJV:

And I saw a new heaven and a new earth: for the first heaven and the first earth were passed away; and there was no more sea. 2 And I John saw the holy city, new Jerusalem, coming down from God out of heaven, prepared as a bride adorned for her husband. 3 And I heard a great voice out of heaven saying, Behold, the tabernacle of God is with men, and he will dwell with them, and they shall be his people, and God himself shall be with them, and be their God. 4 And God shall wipe away all tears from their eyes; and there shall be no more death, neither sorrow, nor crying, neither shall there be any more pain: for the former things are passed away. 5 And he that sat upon the throne said, Behold, I make all things new. And he said unto me, Write: for these words are true and faithful. 6 And he said unto me, It is done. I am Alpha and Omega, the beginning and the end. I will give unto him that is athirst of the fountain of the water of life freely. 7 He that overcometh shall inherit all things; and I will be his God, and he shall be my son. 8 But the fearful, and unbelieving, and the abominable, and murderers, and whoremongers, and sorcerers, and idolaters, and all liars, shall have their part in the lake which burneth with fire and brimstone: which is the second death. 9 And there came unto me one of the seven angels which had the seven vials full of the seven last plagues, and talked with me, saying, Come hither, I will shew thee the bride, the Lamb's wife. 10 And he carried me away in the spirit to a great and high mountain, and shewed me that great city, the holy Jerusalem, descending out of heaven from God, 11 Having the glory of God: and her light was like unto a stone most precious, even like a jasper stone, clear as crystal; 12 And had a wall great and high, and had twelve gates, and at the gates twelve angels, and names written thereon, which are the names of the twelve tribes of the children of Israel: 13 On the east three gates; on the north three gates; on the south three gates; and on the west three gates. 14 And the wall of the city had twelve foundations, and in them the names of the twelve apostles of the Lamb. 15 And he that talked with me had a golden reed to measure the city, and the gates thereof, and the wall thereof. 16 And the city lieth foursquare, and the length is as large as the breadth: and he measured the city with the reed, twelve thousand furlongs. The length and the breadth and the height of it are equal. 17 And he measured the wall thereof, an hundred and forty and four cubits, according to the measure of a man, that is, of the angel. 18 And the building of the wall of it was of jasper: and the city was pure gold, like unto clear glass. 19 And the foundations of the wall of the city were garnished with all manner of precious stones. The first foundation was jasper; the second, sapphire; the third, a chalcedony; the fourth, an emerald; 20 The fifth, sardonyx; the sixth, sardius; the seventh, chrysolyte; the eighth, beryl; the ninth, a topaz; the tenth, a chrysoprasus; the eleventh, a jacinth; the twelfth, an amethyst. 21 And the twelve gates were twelve pearls: every several gate was of one pearl: and the street of the city was pure gold, as it were transparent glass. 22 And I saw no temple therein: for the Lord God Almighty and the Lamb are the temple of it. 23 And the city had no need of the sun, neither of the moon, to shine in it: for the glory of God did lighten it, and the Lamb is the light thereof. 24 And the nations of them which are saved shall walk in the light of it: and the kings of the earth do bring their glory and honour into it. 25 And the gates of it shall not be shut at all by day: for there shall be no night there. 26 And they shall bring the glory and honour of the nations into it. 27 And there shall in no wise enter into it any thing that defileth, neither whatsoever worketh abomination, or maketh a lie: but they which are written in the Lamb's book of life.

Revelation 22:1-21 KJV:

And he shewed me a pure river of water of life, clear as crystal, proceeding out of the throne of God and of the Lamb. 2 In the midst of the street of it, and on either side of the river, was there the tree of life, which bare twelve manner of fruits, and yielded her fruit every month: and the leaves of the tree were for the healing of the nations.

3 And there shall be no more curse: but the throne of God and of the Lamb shall be in it; and his servants shall serve him: 4 And they shall see his face; and his name shall be in their foreheads. 5 And there shall be no night there; and they need no candle, neither light of the sun; for the Lord God giveth them light: and they shall reign for ever and ever. 6 And he said unto me, These sayings are faithful and true: and the Lord God of the holy prophets sent his angel to shew unto his servants the things which must shortly be done. 7 Behold, I come quickly: blessed is he that keepeth the sayings of the prophecy of this book. 8 And I John saw these things, and heard them. And when I had heard and seen, I fell down to worship before the feet of the angel which shewed me these things. 9 Then saith he unto me, See thou do it not: for I am thy fellowservant, and of thy brethren the prophets, and of them which keep the sayings of this book: worship God. 10 And he saith unto me, Seal not the sayings of the prophecy of this book: for the time is at hand. 11 He that is unjust, let him be unjust still: and he which is filthy, let him be filthy still: and he that is righteous, let him be righteous still: and he that is holy, let him be holy still. 12 And, behold, I come quickly; and my reward is with me, to give every man according as his work shall be. 13 I am Alpha and Omega, the beginning and the end, the first and the last. 14 Blessed are they that do his commandments, that they may have right to the tree of life, and may enter in through the gates into the city. 15 For without are dogs, and sorcerers, and whoremongers, and murderers, and idolaters, and whosoever loveth and maketh a lie. 16 I Jesus have sent mine angel to testify unto you these things in the churches. I am the root and the offspring of David, and the bright and morning star. 17 And the Spirit and the bride say, Come. And let him that heareth say, Come. And let him that is athirst come. And whosoever will, let him take the water of life freely. 18 For I testify unto every man that heareth the words of the prophecy of this book, If any man shall add unto these things, God shall add unto him the plagues that are written in this book: **19** *And if any man shall take away from the words of the book of this prophecy, God shall take away his part out of the book of life, and out of the holy city, and from the things which are written in this book.* **20** *He which testifieth these things saith, Surely I come quickly. Amen. Even so, come, Lord Jesus.* **21** *The grace of our Lord Jesus Christ be with you all. Amen.*

About the Author

K. E. Vonn s a licensed minister with over 40 years experience in ministry and an equal amount of experience in the marketplace, having a BS in Business Administration and a MA in Ministerial Leadership. "I am a student of the most fascinating, life-giving book that has ever been written, the Bible; and I have a passion for taking the practical things in life and using them to unveil spiritual truths about God. I am a believer in Jesus Christ but more importantly he is a believer in me."

Subscribe to my newsletter:

✉ https://www.subscribepage.com/KEVonnLanding

Made in the USA
Las Vegas, NV
01 November 2022

58584509R00111